Withdrawn

We Begin in Gladness

Also by Craig Morgan Teicher

Poetry

> *The Trembling Answers*
> *Ambivalence and Other Conundrums*
> *To Keep Love Blurry*
> *Brenda Is in the Room and Other Poems*

Fiction

> *Cradle Book*

As Editor

> *Once and for All: The Best of Delmore Schwartz*

CRAIG MORGAN TEICHER

WE

BEGIN

IN

GLADNESS

How Poets Progress

Essays

Graywolf Press

This publication is made possible, in part, by the voters of Minnesota through a Minnesota State Arts Board Operating Support grant, thanks to a legislative appropriation from the arts and cultural heritage fund, and a grant from the Wells Fargo Foundation. Significant support has also been provided by Target, the McKnight Foundation, the Lannan Foundation, the Amazon Literary Partnership, and other generous contributions from foundations, corporations, and individuals. To these organizations and individuals we offer our heartfelt thanks.

Published by Graywolf Press
250 Third Avenue North, Suite 600
Minneapolis, Minnesota 55401

www.graywolfpress.org

Published in the United States of America

ISBN 978-1-55597-821-1

2 4 6 8 9 7 5 3 1
First Graywolf Printing, 2018

Library of Congress Control Number: 2018934489

Cover design: Kapo Ng

Cover art: Shutterstock

For Robert Farnsworth and Kathleen Reilly, my two great teachers:

Nor is there singing school but studying
Monuments of its own magnificence
                        —W. B. Yeats

In a dark time, the eye begins to see
                        —Theodore Roethke

Contents

Even if you are on the first step, you ought
to be dignified and happy.
To have got this far is no small thing;
what you have done is a glorious honor.
Even that first step, even the first,
is very far removed from the common lot.
In order for you to proceed upon this stair
you must claim your right to be
a citizen of the city of ideas.

—*Constantine Cavafy, "The First Step"*

We Begin in Gladness

Introduction: We Begin in Anticipation

1.

> I thought of Chatterton, the marvellous Boy,
> The sleepless Soul that perished in his pride;
> Of Him who walked in glory and in joy
> Following his plough, along the mountain-side:
> By our own spirits are we deified:
> We Poets in our youth begin in gladness;
> But thereof come in the end despondency and madness.

These famous lines come from William Wordsworth's long, essayistic poem "Resolution and Independence." Robert Lowell revisits the lines in his poem "To Delmore Schwartz," from *Life Studies*, in which he ascribes to Schwartz a chilling play on Wordsworth's closing couplet:

> You said:
> *"We poets in our youth begin in sadness;*
> *thereof in the end come despondency and madness;*

Both versions point to an old, sad stereotype about poets: that, perhaps, writing poems and looking too long at the trials of the human mind and heart in a troubled world beckon poets to their undoing.

Lowell and Schwartz were thinking particularly of their own imperiled peers—Sylvia Plath, Randall Jarrell, and John Berryman most famously—who met terrible ends in the throes of mental ill health. Poetry couldn't save them, Schwartz seems to say.

But many poets—Wordsworth was among them—live and write into ripe old age and have the chance to author what can be a remarkable literary product, late work, the result of a lifetime's artistic development. Of the prose writer Primo Levi, whose suspected suicide was a frightening and disheartening cap to his life's work, the critic Joan Acocella writes, "It is a species of sentimentality to think that the end of something tells the truth about it." She means that artists' lives do not necessarily parallel their art, or even indirectly cause it—Wallace Stevens, for example, wrote little poetry about his day job as an insurance executive. It's a misapprehension to read by their deaths—or even by their lives, in many cases. To read them, however, by their journeys, by how their art grew and changed over the course of their writing lives, tells us a great deal about what they made and why.

Poetry is a conversation, an extended one, occupying, perhaps, the span of an entire life. Poets converse, first and foremost, with their language—English for our purposes—and with the idea of language itself. Poets are word fetishists, among other things, and their grounding belief is that language is humankind's greatest technology, inexhaustible, endlessly adaptable, a mirror of a poet's own time and, hopefully, of the endless unfolding of all time. A poet casts words into the ether to hear what words come back. It can seem like a lopsided dialogue, only part of the conversation. But most poets will tell you that's not the case: poets speak inwardly, talking into their minds and listening for their minds' responses. Each word is followed by another, each sentence answered by a sentence; each stanza opens into the next, and, when poems are working, they are full of discoveries, thoughts poets didn't know they had, thoughts, perhaps, they hadn't had until that moment, which are encoded in the language itself, which poets have trained themselves to hear.

The language, in the way I'm referring to it, is made up of many things—all the speech and text poets have heard throughout their lives: conversations, schooling, the poetry of the present and the past, and all the elements of culture—music, sports, film, TV, digital media, art—that have helped form an individual's personality. Together, these elements create a matrix of connections, which poems can reveal. This is in part what defines a poet's "voice." Using the particulars of the language that formed them, poets hope to tell the truth about their time as exemplified in themselves, in what they see and, more precisely, hear. Whether or not she writes about her own biography, she is the mouth through which her time is sung— they are *her*, *his* words, after all. Poetry makes its case through each poet's sensibilities; it is never impersonal.

Though it seems, at first, like an art of speaking, poetry is an art of listening. The poet trains to hear clearly and, as much as possible, without interruption, the voice of the mind, the voice that gathers, packs with meaning, and unpacks the language the poet knows. It can take a long time to learn to let this voice speak without getting in its way. This slow learning, the growth of this habit of inner attentiveness, is poetic development, and it is the substance of the poet's art. Of course, this growth is rarely steady, never linear, and is sometimes not actually growth but diminishment—that's all part of the compelling story of a poet's way forward.

A poet speaks to him or herself by writing down a line and then converses by listening, by transcribing—with some editing—what comes back. For this conversation to be meaningful and engaging— to others, of course, but most importantly, in the act of composition at least, to the self—it must unfold and change: thoughts must lead to other thoughts. Why would anyone stay in a conversation that never goes anywhere? Good talk is full of surprises, of questions that lead to revelations that prompt further questions. Think of all the great poems that open up this way, as when Emily Dickinson famously plays a game of call-and-response with her mind:

> I'm Nobody! Who are you?
> Are you—Nobody—Too?
> Then there's a pair of us!
> Don't tell! they'd advertise—you know!

We, her future readers, are among those Dickinson is reaching out to with that "you," but to find us, over 150 years into the future, she calls out into the closest thing she's got to a time tunnel: her imagination. And because we can't answer back, she must listen for her mind's own answer, must conjure us in the future imagining her in the past. (I like to think of the "they" as the people of her, and our, present, those who, by choice, leave themselves out of the poetic conversation, who neither speak nor listen with their imaginations as one must to read and write poems.)

Of course, most poems do not take the form of question-and-answer sessions. But, implicitly, poems probe the unknown, beginning on firmer ground and speaking until they have expressed the otherwise inexpressible, something sayable only in those words, in that poem. Poets work to express the questions roiling beneath their statements, the statements beneath their questions. Poets rarely trust assertions.

Because a poet's voice—the literal material of a poet's art—is bound, is limited, by the language and culture that has formed her, she is, more or less, stuck with herself, with *her* self, with *its* words. Despite the near limitlessness of possible poetic styles in which to write, each poet must draw on a personal "word hoard," in Seamus Heaney's figuration. Hence most poets really only have a few subjects, a few linguistic pursuits, that occupy them throughout their writing lives. Most have only a few axes to grind, answers to question, theories to prove.

Wordsworth was obsessed with casting the vernacular of his day in poetry. William Carlos Williams, later, was obsessed with the idea that plainspoken American English could be—*should be*—the stuff of poetry. All Williams's works—whether his urban pastorals; his character studies of the people of Rutherford, New Jersey; his epic professions of love and apology to his wife, Flossie; his poems about paintings or about poetry itself—seek to exemplify that idea above all. More recently, Kevin Young has made a prolific body of work based on the rhythms and movements of blues and jazz, historically black forms of music made in America through which he revisits and revises the texts of African American history.

And yet, despite a relatively narrow range of subjects and/or means, few poets write the same kind of poem throughout a writing life. The poets who write *very* different kinds of poems over the course of their lives are, of course, profound exceptions to this notion of a poet's narrow range—Dickinson, Walt Whitman, William Butler Yeats, Gwendolyn Brooks, Elizabeth Bishop are each many poets in one, which, in part, qualifies them as "major" poets. Seeking to extend their conversation, to home in more precisely on what they believe and feel to be true about language, poets change their poems.

Sometimes this happens deliberately. In the early 1960s, James Wright was disgusted with the way his new poems resembled his old ones, so he went off on a translating jag; he emerged from that period of translating Spanish and German poetry with a new style informed by the poems of Pablo Neruda, César Vallejo, and Hermann Hesse that he'd been translating.

Sometimes the changes transpire somewhat accidentally, as they did with Delmore Schwartz, whose late poems, which follow decades of degrading mental imbalance, are sloppy, strange, and transcendent. Regardless of how development happens, the result is a new kind of poem that the poet didn't know how to write before. Charting the means of these changes is the object of these essays.

2.

Let's say that a poet's development begins with the first evidence that she has "found her voice," in the first poems that show the poet is speaking distinctively, in a way that feels like her own. That's, of course, hard to characterize and identify.

For example, Monica McClure, a young Mexican American poet who is, to my ear, among the most exciting of the rising generation, has found, in her first book *Tender Data*, the beginnings of her mature voice. Her work is set mostly in the hip cultural enclaves of New York City, taking as its ostensible subjects the insider worlds of couture fashion, drugs, and literature; it seems, on first glance, to be a chronicle of hipsters at play. Her poems are also heavy on glancing references to theorists and philosophers (Michel Foucault, Simone Weil, and many others). She uses iPhone-age shorthand and slang aplenty. And her poems are rife with direct challenges to readers who think they "get it."

McClure's poetry naturally combines opposing forces. Mistrust of emotional confession meets strong, earnest emotions and admissions of transgression and triumph; pop culture subjects fill classically crafted poems; a flippant tone belies the poems' ultimate seriousness. Of course none of these elements is new to poetry: the poems are woven of strands of the poetic trends of the last three decades, which in turn took cues from Frank O'Hara's quick jump cuts and non sequiturs, ironic self-appraisals, flirtatious winks toward the reader, cameos from celebrities and pop culture icons, bits of history. But all of it is in service of, or meant to finally direct the eye toward, moments of emotional vulnerability that erupt seemingly out of nowhere, like the sudden burst of popping balloons, and disappear as suddenly.

A few lines from the poem "Luxe Interiority" offer up a sampling of all of this:

> I was starved for love
> Now I've just had an abortion
> It's Mercedes Benz Fashion Week
> but I don't want to go to the shows
> The social worker who performed
> My intake consultation had lined
> Her eyes with Kohl's
> I think I would like to be a part of culture
> While remaining without

How are we to synthesize these contradictions, and how seriously should we take them? The poem never lets us know. The satiated hunger for love seems to result in an unwanted pregnancy, but that hardly preoccupies the speaker, who is equally interested in the social worker's bad makeup and a bid for a lasting place in culture. But even this desire, the poet's longing for immortality, is felt lightly and ambivalently—imagine Dickinson prefacing "I could not stop for death" with "I think." McClure strips the sacred of its holiness in order to make it as accessible—to her and to us—as the secular, the silly. To me, this is evidence of a poet who already knows a great deal about the elements that make up her sensibility in an era when collage is the lingua franca of much contemporary poetry.

Looking closely at these lines by McClure, we can see the various aspects of her voice taking shape. Clearly, her sense of language is casual, spoken, rather than rarefied and literary: "Now I've just had an abortion." The great poetry of the past is here, intimated, for instance, by the formality of the last three words quoted earlier, "While remaining without," which hark back to a time when poetry was always meant to be more rhetorical. McClure has a lot she needs to say and stake a claim to, not least of which is the profundity of her moment's popular culture: "Mercedes Benz Fashion Week" is asserted as proper poetic material simply by its inclusion. Also here, unsubtly so, is the influence of so much contemporary poetry: the associative leaps between the abortion, "the shows," and "The social worker who performed / My intake consultation" are deeply symptomatic of the poetry that's been prominent at least since the 1980s, tactics McClure might have gleaned from the work of Jorie Graham, Lucie Brock-Broido, C. D. Wright, and the many poets who have influenced them and whom they have influenced.

As I said earlier, a poet is also stuck with herself, limited—and enabled—by the elements that shaped her imagination, her vocabulary, and her deployment of language. For McClure, those elements include her Mexican American heritage, her Southern upbringing, and her countercultural life in New York.

I like to use Bob Dylan, one of the most important and influential artists in any medium of the last half century, whose winning the Nobel Prize for Literature in 2016 called into question for many the very definition of literature, as an example of how the limitations of an artist's abilities engender art. Dylan is neither a great guitar player nor a great singer. The greatness of his art is actually built upon, built out of, these two facts. After his first self-titled album, mostly composed of interpretations of seminal folk songs, careful guitar work, at least on Dylan's own part, is not an important part of his art. Nor is a clean and flexible singing voice. By his major mid-1960s albums—*Highway 61 Revisited, Blonde on Blonde*—Dylan is focusing on what he has realized are his strengths: a wildly associative verbal imagination, an encyclopedic knowledge of and ability to recontextualize the folk music tradition, a deep mistrust of authority and the accepted ways of doing things, among others. Dylan's great innovations are in his lyrics themselves, and in his inventive song forms. He realized that he had a knack for penetrating, surreal lyricism, and could write verse after verse all in service of a kind of emotional argument—think of "Ballad of a Thin Man." He also realized he needed to develop an elastic, often epic, song form to accommodate his tidal waves of words. So he began writing extended folk-rock songs, the templates for so much later music, simple alterations of verse and chorus, that build, through the lyric content, to emotional crescendos, though the form itself rarely builds or alters.

He grew his great art as a tangent, departing from expected patterns he realized he could not fulfill—Joan Baez, his friend and collaborator, for instance, was a virtuosic singer, but not an innovator. He was no great singer, but he was a great artist, and he listened to his limitations to figure out how.

The same tends to hold true for poets. McClure has languages and dialects, insider knowledge of hip culture, and deep emotion coursing through her imagination. To find her voice, she's crafted an art from what she has, crafted it against what she doesn't—such as, for instance, a knack for received poetic forms. Her limitations, which are also her preferences and particularities, help define her voice.

3.

Paul Muldoon, in an interview with the *New Zealand Listener*, said, "Poets disimprove as they go on. It's just a fact of life. It's not a pleasant one." I wouldn't say it's quite a fact—plenty of poets get better, or arrive at something new and necessary, in old age: imagine poetry without Yeats's late masterpieces—but I understand what Muldoon is getting at. Some poets—many, even—develop and discover until they hit some point that marks the limit of their powers, or of their will to try to extend those powers. Then they write versions of the same poem over and over again for the rest of their career.

I'm most interested in the ascent, the way a poet climbs to her greatest possible profundity and specificity. That's what we can learn from the most. To understand a poet's disimprovement, we need to understand the height from which she has descended. And, anyway, the best poets don't disimprove at all—they change. Late Lowell is different from middle-period Lowell; his late poems lack the sonic thunder and formal rigor of his middle ones, but they say much we need to hear in ways we need to hear it.

I'll assert that poets develop toward masterpieces, plateaus at which they are able to deploy, with seeming effortlessness, what they have learned to say; great poets become virtuosos of their own voices, their own sensibilities. In a masterpiece, nothing is wanting; the poem is fully achieved; no words could be deleted, and we are arrested in reading it. Masterpieces can occur anytime in a poet's writing life. Some examples include Lowell's early poem "Colloquy in Black Rock," Bishop's "The Fish," and Robert Hayden's "Those Winter Sundays," all poems that were written relatively early in their authors' careers. But Yeats's "The Circus Animals' Desertion," one of his last poems, is another kind of masterpiece, one built upon many previous achievements.

Early masterpieces are the most interesting for our purposes, because they exhibit, at the same time, both mastery and that most curious of early poetic milestones: promise. A promising poet is one whose early works seem to point toward further, greater achievement later. Most poets of promise have not yet written a masterpiece. Their poems, like McClure's, show an already-developed sensibility ready to take off toward unknown heights.

I would say "At Pegasus," the first poem in the first book by

Terrance Hayes, *Muscular Music*, is an early masterpiece, exhibiting Hayes's achievement and his promise together. Hayes began with unprecedented confidence. In later books, including the National Book Award–winning *Lighthead*, Hayes developed a series of original poetic forms (often based on Asian or classical forms) and perfected a voice that combines smooth delivery of emotional vulnerability with references to the idioms of pop music; he has become an exemplary contemporary poet whose style many younger writers aspire to.

At the beginning, in *Muscular Music*, however, all of this is nascent. What was in ample evidence is that confidence, the ability to say whatever needs to be said seemingly without effort or impediment. In "At Pegasus," Hayes imagines his speaker, a heterosexual man, dancing in a gay club; the poem represents a profound, if perhaps controversial, act of empathy. "'I'm just here for the music,' / I tell the man who asks me / to the floor," writes Hayes, professing a comfort with what's going on around him, though not the kind of belonging that would let him fully participate. "But," he continues, "I have held"

> a boy on my back before.
>   Curtis & I used to leap
>   barefoot into the creek; dance

> among maggots & piss,
>   beer bottles & tadpoles
>   slippery as sperm

It takes no small amount of confidence, even presumption, if not bravery, to assume this kind of empathy with a sexual orientation not one's own. The book opens this way to stake out the territory this career will lay complete claim to: a vision of the world in which one can understand difference deeply without co-opting it, without demeaning others, without "othering" anyone else. When Hayes says, at the end of the poem,

> These men know something
> I used to know.

> How could I not find them
> beautiful, the way they dive & spill
> into each other,

> the way the dance floor
> takes them,
> wet & holy in its mouth.

I believe him. Look at the smart line breaks: "How could I not find them" as a question on its own tugs the imagination toward something bigger than a mere appreciation of physical beauty—it suggests a deeper identification, as though Hayes is willing to admit his sexuality—as perhaps all sexuality—is not simply one thing or another. The obvious reference to oral sex in the final line is a similar instance, celebrating an act that many straight men find embarrassing even to mention. This poem, especially since it was written and published in the 1990s by a black man, is, for its time, quietly revolutionary.

A masterpiece is a work in which a poet's subjects and forms are in complete harmony. In such a poem, something undeniable is articulated, as it is in "At Pegasus" when Hayes turns the dance floor into a metaphor for a definitive gay sexual act. Hayes says something true about language, about his time, about himself. And he says something in this poem that has influenced the poets who came after him, giving male poets permission to write about sexuality without having to plant their flags on one or the other side of a gay/ straight divide, or at least to imagine empathetically across it.

4.

In the essays that follow, I discuss various models for poetic development. I begin by asking why and how poets begin writing poems at all, and look at the ars poetica, a poem in which poetry itself is the subject. Next I look at the remarkable surging development of Sylvia Plath, which leads me to other poets whose major developments occurred in sudden breakthroughs. At the center of the book are studies of modes of poetic growth that spring from engagement with other poets' work. How does one poet's masterpiece—John Ashbery's "Self-Portrait in a Convex Mirror"—enable a later poet, Susan Wheeler, to write her own masterful poem in conversation with Ashbery's? How does Merwin overcome his early mimicry of nineteenth-century poetry to establish his distinctive and influential style? How does the work of the contemporary poet francine j. harris illuminate the poetry of the writers who influenced her? Finally, I turn toward endings, and the ways poets rewrite or revisit early poems in late ones. And looking closely at Louise Glück's death-obsessed late work, I investigate how a poet can bring all the threads of her art together through steady development. While these models are by no means exhaustive, I've gleaned them from the poets and poems I love best, the ones that have most deeply influenced my own thinking about poetry. I hope they will spark similar discoveries in, and will offer similar permissions to, others.

I'm wary of the notion that there could be anything like a "handbook" for poetic development—at the core of poetry is the fact that even the same words said by different people can mean different things. Similarly, the same artistic choices made by different people will lead to different destinations. And while imitation in poetry is a necessary part of apprenticeship, it only matters after the point at which new poets diverge from their masters. I do hope, however, that these investigations of various poets' development offer other writers ways of thinking about life and art—and how art and artists—affect one another.

That said, poetry—like speech itself—is learned by imitation. To truly understand the work of a poet, we must, at some deep, interior level, want to *become* them, or, more impossibly, to *have been* them, to inhabit their poems from the inside. Reading Dickinson, I find myself wishing I had been her, lived her life. The same with Whitman, Stevens, Hayden, Lowell, Lucille Clifton, Tomas Tranströmer, and so many others. Reading their poems makes me want to have lived or to be living their lives, to possess their imaginations, their hearts—their poems' sources. There is no way to come closer to that kind of vast empathy than to trace the lines their lives make through their poetry, their poetic development.

Poets begin, ideally, in gladness, but often they begin in darker states—poetry tends to arise as a way forward for those who have something to say that is painful and unutterable by other, more practical, more direct, means. So, if not in gladness, hopefully poets begin in anticipation, with the knowledge that discoveries lie ahead, that the language has things to tell them if only they will listen. Their art grows alongside their attention to the words that roil within them. And hopefully, too, they do not end in sadness, or madness, but having achieved great art for their own time, and perhaps for all time.

1. BEGINNINGS

and

BREAKTHROUGHS

Ars Poetica: Origin Stories

1.

A poem is something that can't otherwise be said addressed to someone who can't otherwise hear it. By this definition, poetry is deeply impractical and deeply necessary. There aren't good words for most things we need to express, and lots of the people we need to say them to are dead or otherwise unavailable. Poets tend to need poems to handle subjects that are complex, subtle, nuanced, even painful, embarrassing, shameful, or simply ridiculous if actually uttered aloud. And so we have always needed poetry, as long as there has been language, and perhaps even before. Language began with poetry, with the idea that *this* means *that*, a word, a sound, can conjure a thing, with the fact that we often need our mouths to point to what's beyond the reach of our hands.

So much of life happens inside our heads, where other people can't see. Language is the fundamental bridge between inner and outer worlds, between people, even neighbors, who are always roadblocked by their skulls. Poetry is how we pay attention to that bridge, how we make sure it doesn't fall, how we maintain it, fix it when it gets rickety.

As long as people communicate, there will always be poets. But how and why do people begin to be poets, and what do they themselves gain from poetry? The people who gravitate toward poetry, usually as children or teenagers, love words, learn a kind of conjuring magic from them, find them as entertaining as toys. But I would wager that most poets, in addition to being word fetishists, finally dedicate themselves to poetry—or find themselves helplessly in its thrall—in order to answer for something deeper and perhaps darker than their passion for words.

Though their art is a refined form of speech, poets know more about silence than they do about sound. They are people who, for any number of reasons, cannot, or at one point could not, speak. Perhaps they have something particular to say, but as often, they are people desperately in need of speech itself. The philosopher and aphorist E. M. Cioran claims, "One does not write because one has something to say but because one *wants* to say something." Poetry seeks to fill the silence to which most poets have a heightened sensitivity. A certain amount of loneliness—an awareness of the unsayable—is a precondition for poetry, or for much poetry. Which is not to suggest most poetry is sad or lonely, just that it must be aware of the space around it, the silence that defines it. This is why poems look the way they do, filling only part of the page. Line breaks and stanza breaks make room for silence, include it in the poem, literally illustrate it.

If poets are the keepers of the unsayable, then silence, not language, is a poet's natural element, the realm where the unsayable lives. Poets fetishize silence as much as words; they are disturbed and comforted by the sounds that interrupt it. This is what John Keats means by *Negative Capability*, his notion of a poet's basic qualification, the need for "being in uncertainties, Mysteries, doubts, without any irritable reaching after fact & reason." This is a fancy way of describing ambivalence, also a basic qualification for a poet, the ability to passionately hold two opposing feelings at once. Poets need ambivalence in order to acknowledge the unsayable and speak nonetheless. The hidden subject of all poems is the silence that surrounds them, the things that can't be, that will never be said; a real poem points to everything beyond it.

2.

Silence is certainly what got me started. I was an only child, almost paralyzingly attached to my mother. I began writing poems at the age of fourteen, just after my mother died. Poetry was an almost instant reaction, as if a symptom of her death. I used to tell her everything, talk to her constantly every day of my life. Poetry was, it is now obvious to me, my response to the shock of suddenly having no one to address everything to. I had nothing in particular to say, but needed to say something, to anyone, to everyone.

So, poetry was a natural fit. And when I began to learn, in my tenth-grade honors English class, of the many people who had devoted their lives to it throughout history, I was hooked. It's a sad origin story, I know, but it has compensated me with a life filled with joy and interest, with a community of brilliant and obsessed people, with objects for my devotion. I think, in broad strokes, mine is a pretty common story of how and why poets begin. My early poems were terrible, but that's beside the point. I was speaking, and that is what mattered, all that matters now. I was speaking out of a silence.

Poets have always loved to write about their beginnings, about what brings them to poetry, about the sense of purpose it gives to their lives. This famous poem by Constantine Cavafy made me proud as a budding teenage poet, and gave me hope:

The First Step
To Theocritus one day the young
poet Eumenes was complaining:
"By now two years have passed since I've been writing

and I've only done a single idyll so far.
It's the only work that I've completed.
O woe is me, I see how high it is,
Poetry's stairway; very high indeed.
And from where I stand, on this first step,
I shall never ascend. Unhappy me!"
Theocritus replied: "The words you speak
are unbecoming; they are blasphemies.
Even if you are on the first step, you ought
to be dignified and happy.
To have got this far is no small thing;
what you have done is a glorious honor.
Even that first step, even the first,
is very far removed from the common lot.
In order for you to proceed upon this stair
you must claim your right to be
a citizen of the city of ideas.
It is difficult, and rare as well,
to be entered into that city's rolls.
In its agora you'll find Legislators
whom no mere adventurer can fool.
To have got this far is no small thing;
what you have done is a glorious honor."

—*Translated by Daniel Mendelsohn*

Poets love to be a little bit haughty about what they do, to make it sound hard. And, of course, it is: time is a harsh judge of poets; it forgets most of them. But what I love about this poem is its sense of camaraderie, of mentorship, of passing the torch. Poets, even, especially, dead ones, mentor each other, as Keats continues to do, teaching the art form to any who wants it. I don't believe poetry is for everyone, that poetry should strive to be more accessible, but I strongly believe that anyone who approaches poetry's gates—and there *are* gates—will find that they will open after a bit of pushing. What "the young / poet Eumenes" has done, this "glorious honor," is not make great art; he has joined a company of practitioners, a maintenance crew; he has found his calling and his community. He has approached the gates, pushed, and stepped inside a world of bewilderment; he fears it will never become a familiar place. To some extent, it won't—it's the realm of the unfamiliar—but as he develops his negative capability, his comfort in ambivalence, Eumenes will find he's home. That's what Theocritus is trying to explain to him; it's what all good teachers of poetry teach. This is how and why poets begin, to find themselves among others who will listen, who want to listen and talk.

Rainer Maria Rilke, in *Letters to a Young Poet*, puts this initiating lesson somewhat more harshly:

> Go into yourself. Examine the reason that bids you to write; check whether it reaches its roots into the deepest region of your heart, admit to yourself whether you would die if it should be denied you to write. This above all: ask yourself in your night's quietest hour: *must* I write? Dig down into yourself for a deep answer. And if it should be affirmative, if it is given to you to respond to this serious question with a loud and simple "*I must*," then construct your life according to this necessity.

Rilke was nothing if not self-important and at times overdramatic—that's one of the charms of his poetry, and one of its risks (read too much Rilke before writing and you'll find yourself writing bad Rilke). He was also endlessly wise, at least in his best writing. This passage haunted and embarrassed me when I first read it as a teenager, and it bit my conscience for years after. Would I die if I stopped writing poems? At that time, the answer was surely no. But

I now think I misunderstood the question. I could have stopped writing and survived, but I could not have stopped speaking, or communicating at least. Words were—and they remain—my lifeline, my way forward, my way of knowing the silence, but not succumbing to it. That is probably true for most people, in some sense. But to be so forgiving and open-ended was not Rilke's style, and it would not have made a good and immortal piece of writing. But poetry should be—no, *is*—available to all who want it, as long as they are willing to apprentice themselves to its strangeness and endure some confusion and ambivalence. In his depths, I think Rilke believed that too.

A poet's apprenticeship begins when he or she starts to recognize this sense of mission, of necessity, when silence and words can live together. And perhaps Rilke's question—will I die?—is ultimately what drives them to the depths of real poetry. But it is a simple and common need that they are trying to fill: not to be alone.

What I'm talking about here is one of poetry's greatest genres: the ars poetica, in which the poet describes his or her reasons for practicing their art. "The First Step" is certainly such a poem, an origin story, and *Letters to a Young Poet* could be seen as an ars poetica in prose. The genre dates back at least to the first century BCE, most notably to a poem called "Ars Poetica" by Horace. The American poet Archibald MacLeish wrote a famous "Ars Poetica," and it is very much concerned with silence: "A poem should be wordless / as the flight of birds," he writes, an understatement, a fallacy, that makes me think of the silence, the need to speak, out of which poetry grows. He also says, "A poem should be equal to: / Not true" and "A poem should not mean / But be." He is talking about those things that can't be said that we need to say, and about the way that poetry can bring them into being, make a fact of them. This is a serious way of putting serious stuff, but not all ars poeticas are so serious.

Czeslaw Milosz has a sort of lighthearted poem called "Ars Poetica?" in which he makes some very serious claims for poetry— "poems should be written rarely and reluctantly, / under unbearable duress"—but uses humor to hold back a bit, to take himself and his art less seriously, to portray his ambivalence:

> What reasonable man would like to be a city of demons,
> who behave as if they were at home, speak in many tongues,
> and who, not satisfied with stealing his lips or hand,
> work at changing his destiny for their convenience?
>
> It's true that what is morbid is highly valued today,
> and so you may think that I am only joking
> or that I've devised just one more means
> of praising Art with the help of irony.
>
> There was a time when only wise books were read,
> helping us to bear our pain and misery.
> This, after all, is not quite the same
> as leafing through a thousand works fresh from psychiatric clinics.

I like to think of poetry as a pasture—rather than Milosz's and Cavafy's cities—where demons can graze, can move around freely, within bounds, munching grass, making mischief and meaning, in a safer place than the streets of my life. Of course, as Milosz points out, they always escape—for Milosz, they were never cordoned off—and make real trouble in the real world. They "work at changing . . . destiny for their convenience"; they make us act badly, hurt others and ourselves, make us live out our fears. They *are* our fears, our feelings, let loose as action. Poetry seeks to help us understand this, perhaps to change or control it, though poetry is not, as Milosz says, psychology, purely intended to help us. He continues:

And yet the world is different from what it seems to be
and we are other than how we see ourselves in our ravings.
People therefore preserve silent integrity,
thus earning the respect of their relatives and neighbors.

The purpose of poetry is to remind us
how difficult it is to remain just one person,
for our house is open, there are no keys in the doors,
and invisible guests come in and out at will.

Perhaps poetry is the best forum in which to acknowledge that "the world is different from what it seems to be," that it is, in its wholeness, unseeable, and so unsayable. But for Milosz, there's something a little funny about all of this, as though the poem tacitly asks, "if we can't see or say what's real, why bother?" And yet we do bother, we must. This is Samuel Beckett's central conflict too—"I can't go on. I'll go on." It's the dark comedy that lets us bear "unbearable duress." It's why many poets are funny, why many comedians are sad. Ambivalence—opposites equally true—is at the core of poetry, and comedy.

Marianne Moore's famous poem "Poetry" is a deeply ambivalent justification for the art form she practiced all her life, with which she struggled deeply. The best-known version of this poem is three lines long, distilled from a much longer poem Moore finally turned against. Here is the short version:

I, too, dislike it.
    Reading it, however, with a perfect contempt for it, one discovers in it, after all, a place for the genuine.

Moore may have been the rare poet who was a word fetishist first and foremost, a collector of words and the unlikely bits of information they carried. What she was after may have been something purer than poetry, a place where she could have her words and nothing else. But we must read her as a poet, and ambivalence, "Reading . . . with . . . contempt," may be the truest sign of love. The "it" in the first line is not poetry as a whole but the esoteric culture that surrounds it, and what people mean when they say, "I just don't understand poetry." (Did Moore's friend Ezra Pound even understand what he meant half the time in the *Cantos*? Perhaps not.) But what I think she believes in, what she likes, is the discovery that happens at the end of the second line—what "one discovers" is the capacity to communicate, to be understood, to use these precise and sinewy sentences (or other kinds of sentences) to reach another person, to accept the silence and the words. What could be more genuine?

Here is another unconventional ars poetica, an abecedary, meaning each line begins with the next letter of the alphabet, by the contemporary poet Mary Szybist, in which she finds a justification for poetry in a happy conversation between two or more kids:

Girls Overheard While Assembling a Puzzle
Are you sure this blue is the same as the
blue over there? This wall's like the
bottom of a pool, its
color I mean. I need a
darker two-piece this summer, the kind with
elastic at the waist so it actually
fits. I can't
find her hands. Where does this gold
go? It's like the angel's giving
her a little piece of honeycomb to eat.
I don't see why God doesn't
just come down and

kiss her himself. This is the red of that
lipstick we saw at the
mall. This piece of her
neck could fit into the light part
of the sky. I think this is a
piece of water. What kind of
queen? You mean
right here? And are we supposed to believe
she can suddenly
talk angel? Who thought this stuff
up? I wish I had a
velvet bikini. That flower's the color of the
veins in my grandmother's hands. I
wish we could
walk into that garden and pick an
X-ray to float on.
Yeah. I do too. I'd say a
zillion yeses to anyone for that.

The question with which this poem opens is a clear example of the difficulty of communicating. Can I ever be sure that when I say "blue," you think of the same color I do? Not really. It takes description, context, and trust to establish common ground. That's the true work of poetry: to bring the inner out, to give my blue to you. "You mean / right here?" Szybist asks. Where? The place where the words are pointing, the thing—or thought or feeling—to which they refer. Szybist teases us in this poem, reminds us how hard it is to communicate what we mean. We can't see the puzzle, "the red of that / lipstick we saw at the / mall," and so we are forced to imagine it, with the help of the clues provided by the poem. It's my puzzle to work out, and yours, and Szybist's too, and where those puzzles overlap, where one interior meets another, and where inner meets outer, is poetry. Who wouldn't want to "suddenly / talk angel?" To a poet, that's a metaphor for being heard in a big way, by everyone, all the distant listeners who otherwise can't hear. Being understood: I, too, would "say a / zillion yeses to anyone for that."

Actually, poetry didn't begin for me with my mother's death; it began much earlier, with the unquenchable urge to speak that made me so close to my mother in the first place. While my friends played baseball or soccer at recess, I longed to find someone to hide with me in the distant corners of the playground and talk. I'd talk about anything—my new alarm clock, my G.I. Joe figures—so long as it was fodder for articulation. Early on, I sensed a magic in bringing my thoughts out into the air. It was a kind of tran-substantiation, metaphor made into fact. Though I'd never have put it that way, that's what I wanted: physicality for my thoughts, not because they were particularly important, but because they were real. By speaking them, I could watch them take shape.

3.

"Clearances VII," part of Seamus Heaney's sequence of sonnets on his mother's death, is not really a sad poem:

> In the last minutes he said more to her
> Almost than in all their life together.
> "You'll be in New Row on Monday night
> And I'll come up for you and you'll be glad
> When I walk in the door . . . Isn't that right?"
> His head was bent down to her propped-up head.
> She could not hear but we were overjoyed.
> He called her good and girl. Then she was dead,
> The searching for a pulsebeat was abandoned
> And we all knew one thing by being there.

The space we stood around had been emptied
Into us to keep, it penetrated
Clearances that suddenly stood open.
High cries were felled and a pure change happened.

How this poem perplexes me, how it intrigues me, how jealous
I am of what it has come to believe in the end: that witnessing a
death is a threshold on the other side of which is some clear new
knowledge. What changes in that moment—at the end of this
Petrarchan sonnet's eighth line, its volta, the formal turn that represents the poem's major emotional event—is that he lets her go,
something almost heroic, superhuman. And maybe it is only in the
imaginative realm of the poem that this is possible.

This is not exactly an ars poetica, but it does suggest one of the
functions of poetry: to clock, record, even enact change in ways
we can't in life. Heaney wrote his share of traditional ars poeticas,
too, like "Personal Helicon," in which he remembers his childhood
fascination with "wells / And old pumps with buckets and wind-
lasses" and connects that early love of the dark mysteries of water
to his adult practice as a poet. Of a well he says:

I savoured the rich crash when a bucket
Plummeted down at the end of a rope.
So deep you saw no reflection in it.

A shallow one under a dry stone ditch
Fructified like any aquarium.
When you dragged out long roots from the soft mulch
A white face hovered over the bottom.

Poets seek reflections, ultimately in words, but, first perhaps, in nature's uncertain mirrors, which send back not an accurate image

of the self but a vision of the world with the self somewhere in it, in a kind of humbling context—"A white face hovered over the bottom"—or with a difference, "echoes [that] gave back your own call / With a clean new music in it." Heaney finds he loves what he can't anticipate, or the surprises he can count on. He recognizes himself and his own mysteries in the unpredictable baggage words carry with them along with his intended meanings. This is why he says "I rhyme / To see myself, to set the darkness echoing." Perhaps, too, this is why he is able to recognize the "pure change" that follows his mother's death—he's been attuning himself to these kinds of changes—"pure," if not always welcome—all along through his poetic practice.

"Clearances VII" features all the sonic lusciousness for which Heaney is most famous: the father's quoted lines are delicious, the rhythmic beckoning of "you'll be in New Row" is seductive, simple, and songlike. And that caesura before "Isn't that right" is like a little hammock for the mind to rest in. Then there is the wonderful interlaced rhyming—glad, head, dead, penetrated—which makes the joy, the grief, and change seem preordained, as though they were an aspect of language itself, of sound, of nature. And of course they are.

The poem's movements are also guided—one might even say steadied, as by a friend at the bedside of the dying—by the long tradition of the sonnet form. The sonnet is mysterious and magical, a little box of fourteen lines in which something vast and complete can nonetheless transpire. This one's loosely Petrarchan, with an octave—the first eight lines at Heaney's mother's bedside, which conclude "Then she was dead"—and a sestet, the last six lines in which the "pure change" dawns and is finally announced. The sonnet form is full of checkpoints like these—the poem's thinking or its narrative must change at the volta; after that, the poet has only a few lines to finish up, all while making sure to hit whatever rhyme scheme has been determined (in Heaney's case, it's a fairly odd one, with the couplet that usually closes a sonnet at the top, and a bumpy network of end words, many of which are near or perfect rhymes). It's a comforting form, predictable by design, yet subtly wired for surprises. It's the perfect form for mourning, which is the slow dawning of painful change, and for epiphany.

I'm happy for the family that they get this moment of intimacy from the otherwise reticent father, but what interests me most is that volta: "He called her good and girl. Then she was dead." The father's soul-baring does nothing to forestall his wife's death. No, she is already dead by the time the sentence is cast, and that is why the change is pure: because the death is apprehended without sentimentality; it is accepted, at least in the language used to express it, to describe it, as it happens. This is why the poem is almost neatly divided in half: Heaney leaves emotion that exceeds its cause behind him after line seven. The remainder of the poem strives to say death cleanly. He admits that the life of the mother "had been emptied / Into us to keep." The mother herself is gone, has been transformed into an aspect of the selves of her mourners. She's become a poem. Rarely does an elegy admit this fact: that the dead vanish completely, and all that is left is a diminished shadow, buttressing for the personalities of those left behind. And so, in that last line, Heaney achieves understanding of what death is, what words are necessary for letting go.

Perhaps because my mother died when I was young, I still believe, somewhere very real within me, that if I wait around long enough, I will find myself back in the past, that I will recognize my own "pure change," my coming to poetry. That hope is why this poem sticks in my throat like a bone, and why I write. How I wish I could know what this poem knows. Heaney's wisdom stretches far, far beyond this lovely, enacted insight about grief, but so much of my psyche eddies around my inability to believe it. I am desperate for a "pure change," and I think many others are too. This poem points a way toward such a change, toward what poetry can do.

And yet—and here is why it's poetry, not memoir—death happens, matter-of-factly, but as it can only in art, laced with a bit of drama. It's the opposite of transcendence, no angel rising from the corpse, no consolation from beyond, beyond the meaning the family makes of the father's naked expression of his simple love. And yet something beyond expression occurs, something worth straining after in words, something one cannot get over. Death is made meaningful, though the meaning is never quite clear—it's something unsayable addressed to someone who can't hear.

Or perhaps the meaning is heard and understood—by us, the distant readers in the room beyond the mother's—and even Heaney's—death, though it's not something we could paraphrase or explain, except in another poem. This meaning, which is heard in silence, is what Moore is referring to as "the genuine"; it's Cavafy's "glorious honor," the reminder that is Milosz's "purpose of poetry," what Szybist says her "yeses" to. When we hear and understand what can't be said and heard, that's when "a pure change" happens. It's what poets go in search of, what they write toward, why one poem, one kind of poem, isn't enough—the unsayable is never quite said.

Sylvia Plath's Surges

The voluminous critical conversation about Sylvia Plath has tended to orbit a few topics: her suicide, of course, and the ways mental illness and madness perhaps predicted her death and marked her poetry; the blazing ferocity of her posthumous masterpiece *Ariel*; the co-opting of images and metaphors (from the Holocaust, for instance) in those late poems; and the overall relationship of her biography to her supposedly confessional poems, especially when it comes to Ted Hughes, his affair with Assia Wevill, and his curation of Plath's legacy after her death. These are all compelling topics, and they've had a deep and lasting effect on how we read Plath's poetry. But I prefer to think about Plath's amazing poems and the creative surges that enabled her to write them.

In Plath we have a unique example of rapid, surging development of a poet's art. In only seven years—from 1956, when the first poems in her *Collected Poems* were written, to 1963, the year of her death—Plath went from being an obviously talented and excruciatingly ambitious (as her journals attest) apprentice poet with lots of technique and intensity but few real subjects on which to train those powers, to the author of unprecedented works of genius. In Plath's first book, *The Colossus and Other Poems*, the only book of poetry she published in her lifetime, we have an unusual opportunity to pinpoint the moments when her art surges forward in particular poems—we can actually watch her grow as an artist, see a little bit how the magic trick was done, and perhaps learn from it. Plath's earlier poems have a lot to teach about how poets expand their capacities, how they "find" a voice by listening closely to their own minds, and how genius can be, if not made, then at least willfully courted.

Plath was a poet who developed by breakthrough. She worked at poetry as a craftsperson, a wildly driven one; she sat down every day and made herself write, and churned the products of her writing until they became fulfilled poems. In his introduction to her *Collected Poems*, Hughes writes, "To my knowledge, she never scrapped any of her poetic efforts. With one or two exceptions, she brought every piece she worked on to some final form acceptable to her, rejecting at most the odd verse, or a false head or a false tail. Her attitude to her verse was artisan-like: if she couldn't get a table out of the material, she was quite happy to get a chair, or even a toy. The end product for her was not so much a successful poem, as something that had temporarily exhausted her ingenuity." Hughes's characterization of Plath as an artisan feels accurate: even in her minor poems, there's a sense of rightness that pops up at times when the language seems to click into place. There are no rough edges in Plath's early work: all of it feels *worked over*. The poems feel distinctly like aesthetic objects, like word sculptures designed to provoke particular responses in their readers. Whatever Plath encounters in her early poems—a landscape, a creature, a phenomenon of weather, a person out of a mythical past—she renders with exhaustive intensity and precise laborious description. Few poems go by without the inclusion of obscure words—"skinflint trees"; "faces / Lucent as porcelain"; "A rise in the landscape, hummock or hogback." Of course we marvel at the ease with which she deploys her considerable vocabulary—and the poems *are*, always, beautiful—but these words, and so many of the flowery descriptions, seem to be there, in part, to impress, or for the fun of using a new tool she has discovered in her toolbox.

Plath is testing herself, but the early poems mostly show a virtuosity of technique rather than of emotion.

Her hard work honed her sentences and lines—the technical aspects of poetry that actually can be practiced and taught—and kept the floodgates open in case something important was ready to flow through. She came to poetry with an innate sense of the music of words and sentences, and her earliest poems are already taut with the intensity of her personality and her mature work. "With such blight wrought on our bankrupt estate, / What ceremony of words can patch the havoc?" concludes "Conversation Among the Ruins," the sonnet that opens the *Collected*; it's a meditation on a decayed place as a representation of a decaying person, as bleak and unforgiving as she would ever be. "Blight" and "wrought" clang against each other like little swords, her ears attuned. And she had studied up on strict form, still a prerequisite for poetry in the 1950s, and could already deploy rhyme and meter with seeming ease. But it would take her years—though not *that many* years—to find subjects suitable to her voice and craft, subjects that would push and then exceed the frames of her technique.

During her lifetime, Plath published two literary works for adults: *The Colossus and Other Poems*, and her novel *The Bell Jar* (under the pseudonym Audrey Lucas), and she was in the advanced stages of preparing the groundbreaking *Ariel* when she died. She had two major developmental surges in poetry, one on display in each of her major poetry books, *The Colossus* and *Ariel*. The chronologically organized *Collected Poems* shows her searching and working toward those breakthroughs.

Many young poets today, who submit their manuscripts to annual contests year after disheartening year, will relate to the story of the publication of *The Colossus*: Plath submitted an ever-changing sheaf of poems to first-book contests ("three months till the Yales open," she wrote in her journal, psyching herself up to submit to the Yale Younger Poets Prize) and publishers' slush piles during the first years of her marriage to Hughes in England and the United States, saw it rejected, swapped old poems out and new ones in, and sent it out again. Meanwhile, Hughes's debut, *Hawk in the Rain*, won one of those contests, and he was off and running by the time they came to the States. And Plath was excited for him, writing in her journal, "I knew there would be something like this to welcome us to New York! We will publish a book-[s]helf of books between us before we perish! And a batch of brilliant healthy children!" Alas, it would be a narrow shelf in her case, though a deep one. It was during these frustrating and exciting years that something extraordinary began to happen in her work, making the published version of *The Colossus* an uneven and unusually promising book.

Plath and Hughes left England in 1957 and took up residence in Northampton, Massachusetts, where Plath taught at Smith and the couple spent fruitful time at the artist colony Yaddo. "Of course Henry Holt rejected my book last night with the most equivocal of letters. I wept, simply because I want to get rid of the book, mummify it in print so that everything I want to write now doesn't get sucked in its maw. Ted suggested I write a new book. All right, I shall," she writes in her Yaddo journal in 1959. Then, with this in mind, at Yaddo, the *Colossus* breakthrough began: she wrote a clutch of new poems that would open the door. These included "The Colossus," "The Manor Garden," and "Poem for a Birthday," poems she identified as different from her others. At this point, her first manuscript was still making the rounds. These new poems excited her so much she actually thought they were the beginning of a new book that would lay to rest the old manuscript that, she wrote, "feels dead to me." But, "If I were accepted by a publisher," she wrote in her journal before *The Colossus* was taken, "I would feel a need to throw all my new poems in to bolster the book." That is exactly what she did, and why we have the chance to see a new, wilder Plath emerging from the more careful and mannered one. *The Colossus*, composed of the older poems and the newer ones thrown in, was finally accepted and published in England, to which the couple had returned in 1960. Most of the old poems are like "Sow," composed in 1957, in which Plath trains her gaze on a neighbor's "great sow," whose piglets she sees

Shrilling her hulk
To a halt for a swig at the pink teats. No. This vast
Brobdingnag bulk

Of a sow lounged belly-bedded on that black compost,
Fat-rutted eyes
Dream-filmed. What a vision of ancient hoghood must

Thus wholly engross
The great grandam!—our marvel blazoned a knight,
Helmed, in cuirass,

Unhorsed and shredded in the grove of combat
By a grisley-bristled
Boar, fabulous enough to straddle that sow's heat.

Already Plath can render anything with stultifying intensity, and she's gained the control of where to break her lines, her poet's timing, that will make the *Ariel* poems so searing and sinister. But, finally, this poem adds up to little more than a prolonged, overfancy exclamation of, "Wow! That's a really big pig!"

Things get fairly ridiculous pretty quickly: a kind of chivalrous sex scene begins to unfold in the pig pen next door, but we're still just looking at a pig, albeit a highly elevated one. The stakes of the subject are far lower than the stakes in the words that describe it. This poem is not extraordinary, except inasmuch as it shows Plath's already considerable chops; "Sow," along with many of the other *Colossus* poems, is apprentice work.

Elsewhere, in the more famous "Point Shirley," from 1959, we see Plath's exquisite sentences hard at work describing the goings on at her dead grandmother's house. This is a transitional poem, written around the time Plath made an important, tremendous leap, which Hughes recognizes in his introduction to the *Collected*: "This decision to start a new book 'regardless,' and get rid of all that she's written up to then, coincided with the first real breakthrough in her writing, as it is now possible to see." "Point Shirley" is a poem she treasured. She records the writing of it in her journal from 1959: "Finished a poem this weekend, Point Shirley, Revisited, on my grandmother. Oddly powerful and moving to me in spite of the rigid formal structure. Evocative. Not so one dimensional":

> She is dead,
> Whose laundry snapped and froze here, who
> Kept house against
> What the sluttish, rutted sea could do.
> Squall waves once danced
> Ship timbers in through the cellar window;
> A thresh-tailed, lanced
> Shark littered in the geranium bed—
>
> Such collusion of mulish elements
> She wore her broom straws to the nub.

"Point Shirley" holds on to many of the old mannerisms while beginning to allow in a new kind of abandon. It's an elegy for her grandmother, who is embodied by the house she left behind after her death twenty years before. It's a little like "Sow" in its excessively intense descriptive tendencies—with its "sluttish, ruttted sea," for example. The harsh music of "sluttish" and "rutted" raking across that comma is an effect from which Plath would wring great drama and even comedy in later poems, though without the overtly baroque word choice. There are classic Plathian lines—"A labor of love, and that labor lost," for instance, is a particularly concise way of summarizing how human efforts are always undone by nature, and a wink at the Bard. But she still sometimes overdoes it in places where the pluck of the language is more interesting than its meaning—"mulish elements," "Bones, bones only, pawed and tossed," "that spumiest dove"; the sound is wonderful but the sense seems to be making a big deal out of a small moment.

Yet something new is happening. In the lines "I would get from these dry-papped stones / The milk your love instilled in them," I hear a preview of the poem "The Colossus," in which a stone statue becomes the life-giving (and life-taking) body of the beloved. The physical landscape and its objects are beginning to take on the projected life of the poem's speaker in a dramatic way—the act of looking, and the distortions of Plath's poetic language (there is distinct longing for a mother, for instance, encoded in those "dry-papped stones")—are beginning to show the particular peculiarities of Plath's mind, to describe *her* rather than what she sees.

But, in poems written the same year as "Point Shirley," this phenomenon accelerates, and it points the way toward the poet Plath was about to become—in those few poems that crept into the manuscript for *The Colossus*, this excruciatingly intense gaze that Plath has honed begins to become not just the poems' tool, but their subject. The major development kicks off—and we can actually witness the moment it happens, can pinpoint the very line—in "The Eye-mote." Plath's speaker "stood looking / At a field of horses," their

> Tails streaming against the green
> Backdrop of sycamores. Sun was striking
> While chapel pinnacles over the roofs,
> Holding the horses, the clouds, the leaves
>
> Steadily rooted though they were all flowing
> Away to the left like reeds in a sea
> When the splinter flew in and stuck my eye,
> Needling it dark.

We think we're reading a poem about horses, whose object is to describe them with extreme attention as she had done with the sow and her grandmother's house. How slyly Plath pulls the rug out from under us, how suddenly she changes course on the other side of a line break. How could we anticipate "When the splinter flew in"? We're as shocked and as slow to adjust as she is. Once that splinter's flown into her writing, nothing's quite the same again. Suddenly, the poem—and with it, her poetry—is no longer about horses but the fact that the speaker sees

> A melding of shapes in a hot rain:
> Horses warped on the altering green,
>
> Outlandish as double-humped camels or unicorns,
> Grazing at the margins of a bad monochrome.

The poem's subject is no longer what's being looked at but the looking itself, or, more precisely, the strained psyche behind the eyes that distorts what's being seen. Plath's extraordinary verbal inventiveness has begun to find a subject equal to it: the limitless shape-shifting the mind exerts on the world, the ways the heart can inflect, even infect, what happens. "The Eye-mote" is an accidental ars poetica, a poem in which Plath teaches herself how to write and us how to read her poetry. She follows up and extends it in the poem "The Colossus," her first masterpiece, in which she creates a literal monolith, a giant ruined statue, to stand in for the father who died in her childhood:

> Perhaps you consider yourself an oracle,
> Mouthpiece of the dead, or of some god or other.
> Thirty years now I have labored
> To dredge the silt from your throat.
> I am none the wiser.
>
> Scaling little ladders with gluepots and pails of Lysol
> I crawl like an ant in mourning.
> Over the weedy acres of your brow
> To mend the immense skull-plates and clear
> The bald, white tumuli of your eyes.

No wonder Plath titled her first book after this poem—it's incredible, a complete poetic invocation of an emotional knot the speaker can't untie. The father-statue is beyond overwhelming, a father figure who looms so large it's impossible to see him all at once, to interpret his meaning—"Thirty years now I have labored / To dredge the silt from your throat." Plath's speaker has made a kind of home within this lifeless giant—she eats her lunch on a nearby hill amidst his bones; she curls up in his ear to escape the weather. Do the stakes get any higher than this? To admit to oneself that one's life is wholly determined by the unknowable mystery of a lost father—and to craft such a vivid metaphor for this admission? She cleans and glues and works, dwarfed by her project "like an ant in mourning."

The language is so rich, so varied, and so perfectly tuned. Notice how the tone is looser here, with none of the strained over-descriptivness of "Sow" or "Point Shirley." A sense of urgency, real stakes, relieves Plath of her anxiety about making a good poem. She doesn't seem like she's trying or showing off; rather it feels like she's channeling, watching, recording a scene that has unfolded in her mind countless times, albeit with all her poet's tools at the ready. She even brings in brand-name products—"Lysol"—and contemporary things—"gluepots," and a lunchbox—everyday items that would have been beneath the notice of her more elevated earlier poems, but which are essential to conveying the ambivalence and real-person-caught-in-a-dream feel of this one. When she does get fancy ("Mule-bray, pig-grunt and bawdy cackles"), it's in the service of vividness: she wants us to feel the ominous atmosphere around her father-statue, to feel her fear and awe. Is there another image for how the father overshadows and protects the child that is any stranger or more true? I don't think so. Who wouldn't want to climb into their parent's ear? Who would? "The Colossus" is a perfect melding of form and meaning, of craft and art. It's gorgeous, ungainly, frightening, intense, just like the inner life it invokes. "It would take more than a lightning-stroke," she says as if winking at us about what she's accomplished, "To create such a ruin." Lightning struck her imagination, shattering her haunting obsession with her father into this undying metaphor.

The father's death, which occurred in Plath's early childhood, such that she hardly remembered him, becomes the overarching metaphor for the unreachable, for what lies beyond the grasp of life and the living: the dead, and death, of course, but more generally, the imagination, the generative boiling bomb in the depths of her psyche. The growth and development of this image of her father is the marker for the development of her psyche, and of her style. When, in "Daddy," she finally unmoors her father from any notion of reality, it's troubling evidence that there is nothing standing in her imagination's way.

The early Plath was a poet who prized control, who wanted to show she had command of her vocabulary, her tone, her descriptive renderings of what she saw. She was a formalist, like many aspiring poets of her time, and wanted to show her mastery of traditional forms. She treated nearly all her subjects with the same unwavering intensity, which manifests as a kind of poise.

If Plath had stopped before writing the poems that would become *Ariel*, we'd probably still keep a few of these early poems handy—"The Eye-mote" and "The Colossus," especially. Because, aside from the fact that they're great poems, they are unique instances of an artist becoming herself, sounding the depths of her voice, becoming bigger and better in her art than she'd known how to be only a poem or two ago.

But the Plath most readers know and remember, the Plath of *Ariel*, is a poet of extraordinary abandon, who seems singularly out of control, almost at the mercy of her poetry, like someone in the throes of a wild dance. Of course, her art, like a dancer's, is in her ability to carefully and meaningfully choreograph what look like mad flailings. Among the great satisfactions of the *Ariel* poems is their roughness: the roiling that animates Plath's greatest poems requires neither a chair nor a toy, but a wiry, overgrowing vine, an exploding rock, an utter expulsion of propriety, capacities seemingly beyond her control. And to become an artisan-like craftsperson of poems like *that*—well, that's genius, and something we'd never seen before and may never see again.

Breakthroughs

From a bird's-eye view, and in retrospect, we can see that among the forces that shape how particular poets develop as they do, that influence the choices they make, is the mood of the time in which they are writing. Sylvia Plath's inner wildness was constrained by conservative postwar America, when people wanted to appear prosperous and in control of their circumstances. So, Plath's body of work, which appears mannered and orderly, at least until near the end, draws closer and closer to the edge of an inner vortex in which Plath seems to abandon even her own control of what goes on in the poems. As unprecedented as Plath's late poems are, they are also very much a product of their time, the turn of the 1960s, when America began to shed its postwar conservatism and experiment with newer, stranger, more interior identities, which would then inform the ways Americans tried to effect social change in the late 1960s and '70s. All of this is encoded in the poetry of the era.

Three other prominent American poets writing after 1950 can all be seen responding in their poems to the prevailing moods of the years in which they began to write, and all of them experienced breakthroughs in their writing that had to do with breaking out—if only in the imaginative realm of poetry—of social constraints. John Berryman's story parallels Plath's in some ways, except that, of course, he was a man and so was more able to entitle himself to a kind of cultural authority in his poems, though it took him a long time—and a good deal of literary failure—to figure out what to make of that authority. His breakthrough came when he realized he needed to deeply undercut it—to make himself into a kind of literary fool in *The Dream Songs*. James Wright came along a few years later and began as a virtuosic practitioner of the formal midcentury lyric. But, midway through the 1960s, under the influence of galvanizing and free-spirited figures like Robert Bly, who turned his attention to the wilder poets of Latin America and Europe, Wright cast off his formal shackles and mannered tone, becoming a poetic embodiment, in midwestern style, of the burgeoning free spirit of the '60s. He did this in parallel with other major poets, like W. S. Merwin, Adrienne Rich, and Robert Hayden, all of whom paved the way for the surrealist and theory-based experiments of the 1970s and '80s. Then, in the '80s, caught up in the rise of critical theory, and perhaps in response to years of prosperity and cultural opulence, Brenda Hillman, who began as a kind of late confessional poet, shifted in her thinking and writing toward spiritual concerns channeled through increasingly experimental poetry.

This theory of development makes sense mostly from a distance. When we look closer at the lives of these poets, we see that each of their breakthroughs occurred for reasons much closer to home. They wrote in search of truth and surprise, casting off elements of voice and style and adopting new ones when they found themselves saying things they'd already said, writing the same poems over again. Often, this happens early on in a poet's writing life. These three poets let go of an apprentice style in favor of a more mature and surprising one that gave them the ability to surprise themselves, to write what they didn't know they knew.

John Berryman

John Berryman's liminal period, the path to his fundamental break-through, was much longer, stranger, and harder than that of many other poets. Berryman's name may have been familiar to earlier generations of poetry readers who were aware of his early publications in the 1940s, culminating with his first full-length volume, *The Dispossessed*, in 1948, and then *Homage to Mistress Bradstreet* in 1956. Poetry readers today, however, almost entirely associate Berryman with *The Dream Songs*, his monumental long poem composed of 385 short lyrics, which didn't begin to appear until the late 1950s and early '60s, when Berryman was around fifty years old. It's almost as though, as far as most of today's readers are concerned, he wrote nothing before *The Dream Songs*. But why? Most poets of his stature—he did, after all, win the Pulitzer and the National Book Award, and he is now undeniably placed with the major poets of his time—are regarded for early and late works, their development watched closely and studied. But this isn't the case with Berryman.

The Dream Songs was indeed the fulfillment of his art, and the work in which he found his true voice and means of expression, but this late flowering constitutes what seems like such a profound departure from Berryman's earlier poems that it is hard, at first glance, to identify early and late poems as belonging to the same poet. The late poetry—from *77 Dream Songs* on—is wildly exciting, irreverent, funny, crazed, magnetic. The earlier poems simply aren't: many of them sound like undistinguished period pieces, poems in the style of Berryman's more artistically mature peers, Robert Lowell especially, as well as his close friend Delmore Schwartz. My saying this now would have driven the young Berryman mad, as indeed he spent his first decades of writing in a fever of frustration, desperate to catch up and break through.

Take these stanzas from Part I of "A Point of Age," a typical, if strong, poem from *The Dispossessed*:

Images are the mind's life, and they change.
How to arrange it—what can one afford
When ghosts and goods tether the twitching will
Where it has stood content and would stand still
If time's map bore the brat of time intact?
Odysseys I examine, bed on a board,
Heartbreak familiar as the heart is strange.

In the city of the stranger I discover
Strike and corruption: cars reared on the bench
To horn their justice at the citizen's head
And hallow the citizen deaf, half-dead.
The quiet man from his own window saw
Insane wind take the ash, his favourite branch
Wrench, crack; the hawk came down, the raven hovered.

This sounds like nothing so much as "good poetry": it sounds like T. S. Eliot, first, with its dark urban scene. And there's a dash of Schwartz, too, in the generalizing cynicism surrounding this "citizen's head." The rhymes are forceful and fulfilled, and the mood is certainly grim, but there isn't much by which to identify a voice, a particular person or personality at the poem's core. Early poems like this one avoid autobiography: they are like fables, imagining hypothetical man to stand in vaguely for emotions.

One of the great innovations of Berryman's generation was a new centrality given to voice in poetry: the poem could accommodate and make sense of almost any subject, could court almost any amount of nonsense, provided that there is a clear voice—meaning a tone that signals a personality—audible throughout. This is the

magic strategy that allows the otherwise chaotic *Dream Songs* to
hold together, for *The Dream Songs* are defined not so much by a
form or a speaker (though the poems cleave tightly to both) as by
a style, one long sought, which could finally accommodate all the
voices of Berryman's mind and his times:

> —Are you radioactive, pal? —Pal, radioactive.
> —Has you the night sweats & the day sweats, pal?
> —Pal, I do.
> —Did your gal leave you? —What do *you* think, pal?
> —Is that thing on the front of your head what it seems to be, pal?
> —Yes, pal.

But, this feral, multivoiced speaker didn't emerge suddenly and all
at once. Berryman had rehearsed for the part of Henry, his alter
ego in *The Dream Songs*, for years, as Berryman's former student,
Merwin, points out: "The *Dream Songs* present with full assurance
something else that Berryman had been moving toward for three
decades." Berryman developed out of order, putting the pieces of
his voice into place one by one, grinding along slowly, unknowingly
preparing some part of Henry in each of his poetic projects, constantly frustrated with his meager reputation relative to his friends',
finally coming into his own late in his foreshortened life.

At the beginning, he thought he had the patience for a careful
poetic development. In her memoir *Poets in Their Youth*, Berryman's
first wife (of three), Eileen Simpson, recalls his wariness of Schwartz's
sudden fame upon the publication of his debut, *In Dreams Begin
Responsibilities*:

> He didn't envy Delmore his fame. One didn't want success to
> come too early, or too generously. Precocity was an enemy of prom-
> ise. "I must find you a copy of Cyril Connolly's book tomorrow."

In *Enemies of Promise*, Connolly says that fame sets up expectation in critics, and in writers, which restrict a writer's freedom to experiment, to fail, to fall silent. The ideal is to keep almost completely but not entirely underground ("No harm in a *little* encouragement," John said wryly) until one is sufficiently formed and strong enough to be unaffected by either success or, since success can't be constant if one is developing, failure. "Yeats's way was the ideal way. A long slow development, the work getting better, the character stronger, until the late great poems and world fame. That's what Delmore would have wished for himself."

In Dreams Begin Responsibilities was indeed Schwartz's best book, not least because his early renown—he was only twenty-four—put such pressure on him that he never did write as well again. But only Yeats could have been Yeats, a genius at every stage of his "long slow development." Berryman was, alas, not an artist of that order.

While he waited for his "little encouragement," Berryman tried on styles that would lead him, finally, to *The Dream Songs*. The first obvious dream song prototypes are the "Nervous Songs," a series of nine lyrics shaped exactly like the dream songs—three six-line stanzas, though with a more orderly, less intriguing rhyme scheme—spoken in the voices of anxious figures (a professor, a captain, a tortured girl) whose strained psyches are the subjects of the poems. They are probably the high point of *The Dispossessed*. "A Professor's Song" is the most obviously dream song–like:

(. . . rabid or dog-dull.) Let me tell you how
The Eighteenth Century couplet ended. Now
Tell me. Troll me the sources of that Song—
Assigned last week—by Blake. Come, come along,
Gentleman. (Fidget and huddle, do. Squint soon.)
I want to end these fellows all by noon.

The poem begins in the middle of a speech and moves in several registers at once, interior, spoken, addressed to a roomful of students, and also to an imaginary audience in posterity. We feel disoriented, in part because we don't have the materials to understand the lecture, in part because we don't know quite to whom this speaker is talking, and why. Perhaps, too, this speaker sounds like Henry because he sounds like Berryman, who taught undergraduates at Princeton, Harvard, and elsewhere, and certainly shared this speaker's frustration with an uninterested audience. Here Berryman was teaching himself to untether from narrative sense and from the orderly arguments of poems like "A Point of Age."

His next shift occurred in *Sonnets to Chris*, written in the sweaty fury of a love affair as his marriage to Simpson was falling apart. He writes to his lover with longing, seduction, frustration, erudition, mixing registers all the while. This sequence is Berryman's first extended experiment with the serial form, a long poem composed in pieces, which scatter his intensity and voice across many lyric instances. Inconclusiveness is one of the signatures of *The Dream Songs*: Berryman never worries about whether each song's last line packs a punch. Rather, he needs each one to escape its particular corner, like a trapped rat, by its wits. He begins practicing that skill in these sonnets. They're written in a much older style ("They come too thick, hail-hard, and all beside / Smother, necessities of my nights and days, / My proper labour that my storm betrays"), though beginning to show off some fast switching between voices or levels of thought; and *The Dream Songs*, too, would affect a period voice for effect.

Interestingly, and frustratingly for any narrative about poetic development, while Berryman wrote the sonnets in the late 1940s, he wouldn't *publish* them until 1967, after *77 Dream Songs*. Perhaps he was trying to protect his lover, or didn't think the poems were ready—the published collection contains revisions and a few new sonnets, plus an opening poem in the dream song style proclaiming, "*He made, a thousand years ago, a-many songs / for an Excellent lady, wif whom he was in wuv*" (how delicious and dark I find that last phrase, so funny, so self-loathing). It's as if, his breakthrough behind him and his reputation secure, Berryman was ready to show readers how he got there.

Then there is *Homage to Mistress Bradstreet*, acclaimed in the late 1950s as Berryman's first masterpiece, though it is hard to approach it now, detailing as it does a fantastical love between a Berryman-like contemporary speaker and the early American poet Anne Bradstreet. Mostly written in a high diction, it feels classical and stuffy to me, and very little like the mature Berryman. But there is a remarkable moment early in the nearly-thirty-page poem that points the way toward *The Dream Songs'* shifting voices. The poem begins in the poet-speaker's voice, but an unannounced shift occurs between stanzas four and five:

4

Jaw-ript, rot with its wisdom, rending then;
then not. When the mouth dies, who misses you?
Your master never died,
Simon ah thirty years past you—
Pockmarkt & westward staring on a haggard deck
it seems I find you, young. I come to check,
I come to stay with you,
and the Governor, & Father, & Simon, & the huddled men.

5

By the week we landed we were, most, used up.
Strange ships across us, after a fortnight's winds
unfavouring, frightened us;

bone-sad cold, sleet, scurvy; so were ill
many as one day we could have no sermons;
broils, quelled; a fatherless child unkennelled; vermin
crowding & waiting: waiting.

Suddenly Bradstreet is speaking. The transition is unmarked, and it is here that Berryman grasps one of the key strategies of *The Dream Songs*: that the poet's voice encompasses many minds, that the act of imagining is necessarily an act of ventriloquy. The mind moving through its wishes and regrets doesn't explain itself, so why should the poem? It is this insight, along with the serial nature of the sonnets and the thin masks of the nervous songs, that makes a poem like "Dream Song 2" possible. That and decades of stalled ambition, a father who had killed himself, an utterly overbearing mother, and a life of wide reading, all of which were Berryman's, and Henry's, purview:

The jane is zoned! no nightspot here, no bar
there, no sweet freeway, and no premises
for business purposes,
no loiterers or needers. Henry are
baffled. Have ev'ybody head for Maine,
utility-man take a train?

Arrive a time when all coons lose dere grip,
but is he come? Le's do a hoedown, gal,
one blue, one shuffle,
if them is all you seem to réquire. Strip,
ol banger, skip us we, sugar; so hang on
one chaste evenin.

—Sir Bones, or Galahad: astonishin
yo legal & yo good. Is you feel well?

Honey dusk do sprawl.
—Hit's hard. Kinged or thinged, though, fling & wing.
Poll-cats are coming, hurrah, hurray.
I votes in my hole.

It is easy to see the elements of Berryman's earlier poems in evidence here—the shifting voices, especially in the last stanza when we meet Henry's blackface alter ego; the clipped, strained, out-of-order grammar, derived as much from Berryman's intense Shakespeare scholarship (he labored for years over a never-completed critical book about the Bard) as from midcentury entertainment; the fidelity to and mischievousness about form—but what a breakthrough! While Berryman did work his way toward this style, tracing the steps does not fully explain it. He's become a new poet, one less and less like his sources and now entirely like himself.

He would go on working in this style through the two books of *The Dream Songs*, and never quite abandon it in his final two books, which were a kind of denouement, a release valve for the pressure that remained after the dream songs were done.

James Wright

James Wright is famous for his free-flowing, at times almost mystical poems about the Midwest, which he began writing in the early 1960s and which first appeared in the seminal collection *The Branch Will Not Break*. In these poems, horses, fields, old, broken-down buildings, bridges spanning industrial rivers, and moments of solitude figure an expansive—and expanding—if melancholy inner life. They were written alongside the works of other "deep image" poets such as Merwin and Wright's poetic coconspirator Robert Bly, and have been imitated by generations of poets looking for ways to turn the bedrock of their imaginations into the stuff of transcendent poetry. Though the overall tone is often elegiac, many of these poems harbor a kind of optimism, a seductive hope that dawns on them suddenly.

But Wright didn't begin writing this way. In *The Green Wall*, which won the Yale Younger Poets Prize in 1957, selected by W. H. Auden, and in his second volume *Saint Judas* (1959), Wright wrote in what had become a period style for the 1940s and '50s: heavily formal verse colored grimly, filled with self-loathing and fear, and a persistent sense of loss. Take this stanza, from "The Shadow and the Real" in his first book:

> There was no more than shadow where
> She leaned outside the kitchen door,
> Stood in the sun and let her hair
> Loosely float in the air and fall.
> She tossed her body's form before
> Her feet, and laid it down the wall.
> And how was I to feel, therefore,
> Shadow no more than darker air?

These lines, about seeing the promising shadow of a beautiful woman, are lovely, but far from the openhearted announcements of Wright's later poems. While Wright neatly fulfills the rhyme scheme, he does so with a light touch, enjambing the phrases in which his rhymed words appear and picking common words for his rhymes. And there's something sweet and generous in the tone—"She tossed" and "laid" her body and hair, abandoning herself to the wind in a way that suggests Wright's soon-to-blossom sensibility. But hearing later music in earlier songs only works in hindsight; had he not arrived at poems like "A Blessing" a few years later, we'd never look for them here.

Saint Judas, Wright's second book, is in much the same vein, perhaps a darker one. The poems of *Saint Judas* have more "voice" in them, to my ear at least, meaning they've gone from apprentice work, which often feels nascent, a bit like a speaker is still clearing his throat and doing impressions, to the work of a poet who is closer to his own manner. The title poem is gorgeous, powerful, and mysterious, and suggests more than a few of Wright's later themes:

> When I went out to kill myself, I caught
> A pack of hoodlums beating up a man.
> Running to spare his suffering, I forgot
> My name, my number, how my day began,
> How soldiers milled around the garden stone
> And sang amusing songs; how all that day
> Their javelins measured crowds; how I alone
> Bargained the proper coins, and slipped away.
>
> Banished from heaven, I found this victim beaten,
> Stripped, kneed, and left to cry. Dropping my rope
> Aside, I ran, ignored the uniforms:
> Then I remembered bread my flesh had eaten,
> The kiss that ate my flesh. Flayed without hope,
> I held the man for nothing in my arms.

This sonnet about a last, unthinking act of generosity on the part of the man who condemned Christ is, first and foremost, a poem about futility. It makes Judas into a martyr, too, complicating his story. I love the anachronistic use of contemporary detail in the ancient scene—"My name, my number, how my day began"—that acts as a reminder that religious myth is allegorical and elastic. And the casual deployment of that loaded gesture—"Dropping my rope / Aside"—is a soft humanizing of a mythic moment, evidence

of Wright's lightening touch, which he would deploy to greater effect in the future. And who wouldn't envy that last line, how it fits
so neatly in its space, how "for nothing," the poem's essential futility is hidden in the midst of the simple action-sentence, "I held the
man . . . in my arms," an echo of the pietà. It's a great poem, but
Wright still hasn't found the tone and idiom that would carry him
through his even greater work.

This is where the story of Wright's poetic development gets
really fun. In 1961 Wright sent to Wesleyan University Press a manuscript for his third book. He describes the manuscript to Donald
Hall: "It consists of three sections: academic (or, perhaps, formal
or traditional) poems; some three or four monologues etc. which
I call 'fictitious voices'; and then a number of new poems, which
perhaps I will call Explorations, or Experiments, or Open Poems."
This last group contains the first examples of Wright's mature style.
Wesleyan accepted the book, though it was never published—the
same year, Wright withdrew it, excited about "new poems [that] are
sometimes crazier than hell," with which he knew he could soon
fill a book. His art was changing and he didn't want his next book
to have one foot still in his old style.

So what happened? Through his friendship with Bly, on whose
farm Wright spent time writing and reading, and in correspon-
dence with Hall, James Dickey, and others, Wright was beginning
to feel a pull toward a new way of writing, or at least a pull away
from his old one. To his high school English teacher, Elizabeth
Willerton Esterly, with whom he corresponded throughout his
life, he wrote, "Bly . . . is a wild man, a great man I think, who
returned from Norway a couple of years back with the idea that
Americans have been writing too many iambic poems. Bly knows
Scandinavian, German, French, Spanish, Italian. . . . And My God!
What a teacher Bly is!" He continues: "I've gone as far as I want to
go, for the time being, with iambics in *Saint Judas*. So now I am a

writer of free verse, a surrealist, and, most deeply in absorption and interest, a translator." For Wright, the lightning bolt that broke him open to his freer poems—though it took a couple of years, as inner surges often do—was the translation he started doing from Spanish and German poets.

His letters are stuffed with references to the poets he was translating—Juan Ramón Jiménez, Jorge Guillén, Pablo Neruda, Georg Trakl, César Vallejo, Hermann Hesse, and others. In his *Above the River: The Complete Poems*, between *Saint Judas* and *The Branch Will Not Break*, there is a book's worth of translations, though they were not then published as a stand-alone book, but in various anthologies. In these versions of other voices, we hear the first strong glimmerings of Wright's mature style. He would let these other voices lead him to his own.

Look at these lines from Wright's version of "I Want to Sleep" by Guillén, which sound more like the Wright to come than Wright's earlier poems do:

Emptiness, O paradise
Rumored about so long:
Sleeping, sleeping, growing alone
Very slowly.

Darken me, erase me,
Blessed sleep,
As I lie under a heaven that mounts
Its guard over me.

Earth, with your darker burdens,
Drag me down,
Sink my being into my being:
Sleep, sleep.

The voice here has a wishful forward motion, a calling out to the world that is absent in *The Green Wall* and only vaguely hinted at in "Saint Judas." This "heaven that mounts / Its guard over me" feels like the real sky, albeit inflected with the imagination's longing, rather than the mythic heaven from which Judas was "banished." Though Wright says to Esterly that he is becoming "a surrealist," in fact, it is the real that begins to enter his poems now: through these translations, the landscape before his eyes, rather than an imaginary one, becomes the taking-off point for poetry's flights. Nor is the longing as dark as it was. If "I Want to Sleep" is a death wish, it is a gentle and, if possible, a hopeful one—"Sink my being into my being." Even at his most grim, the maturing Wright holds out hope, at least in the power of description, for redemption.

And here are two stanzas from Wright's version of "De Profundis," published in Wright and Bly's 1961 edition of *Twenty Poems of Georg Trakl.* An early twentieth-century Austrian poet who was profoundly important to Wright, Trakl also had a strong influence on the voice Wright ultimately arrived at:

> I am a shadow far from darkening villages.
> I drank the silence of God
> Out of the stream in the trees.
>
> Cold metal walks on my forehead.
> Spiders search for my heart.
> It is a light that goes out in my mouth.

These ragged lines—which borrow their meter from speech rhythms, use all manner of dark, surreal, and suggestive metaphors, and locate the self not in the actual world, but in a shifting landscape of emotionally charged figures—are nothing like the careful surfaces of "The Shadow and the Real." These are moves American poets simply didn't yet have, though, largely through Wright and Bly's efforts, they would become the lingua franca of American poetry from the sixties onward.

These translations more than hint at Wright's "A Blessing," one of the most famous poems from his breakthrough volume *The Branch Will Not Break*:

> Just off the highway to Rochester, Minnesota,
> Twilight bounds softly forth on the grass.
> And the eyes of those two Indian ponies
> Darken with kindness.
> They have come gladly out of the willows
> To welcome my friend and me.
> We step over the barbed wire into the pasture
> Where they have been grazing all day, alone.
> They ripple tensely, they can hardly contain their happiness
> That we have come.
> . . . .
> Her mane falls wild on her forehead,
> And the light breeze moves me to caress her long ear
> That is delicate as the skin over a girl's wrist.
> Suddenly I realize
> That if I stepped out of my body I would break
> Into blossom.

This poem resembles "I Want to Sleep" and "De Profundis" far more than it does "Saint Judas." Note the jagged lines, the long, relaxed phrases between line breaks: "We step over the barbed wire into the pasture / Where they have been grazing all day, alone." There is nothing fancy here; Wright takes his time, lets the scene unfold, lets us walk out into it to meet the horses walking toward him and us. When imagination does begin to inflect the description ("They ripple tensely, they can hardly contain their happiness / That we have come"), it only lifts off from the real slightly, in the service of conveying emotion—in fact, it is Wright who cannot contain his happiness. It surfaces in lyrical language, a music of wishing. Wisdom is born where observation and imagination meet, where the real and ideal touch; the climactic moments here stage such a meeting: "They bow shyly as wet swans. They love each other. / There is no loneliness like theirs." Indeed, love is lonely, the lover both mirror and other. When the epiphanic final line comes, though it is both conditional ("if I stepped") and impossible, we believe it completely, knowing exactly what the speaker feels, the sense that one's inner life has suddenly overwhelmed one's body, a moment when, as Bishop says in "The Map," "emotion too far exceeds its cause."

As this new direction was blossoming out of his translation work, Wright wrote to the poet W. D. Snodgrass, "I . . . started to feel glib, so I said, the hell with it, and leaped into another part of the forest. I do not know how things are working out *as poems*. But I will say this: I feel alive with them, and I am *seeing* (even though I'm not conveying, communicating) things that I never saw before. And, though it sounds (and probably is) immoral, I am having a hell of a good time with poetry. I had lost that, and to get it back is worth everything." Fun—or excitement—is one sure symptom of a developmental surge.

By 1963, when *The Branch Will Not Break* was published, only four years after *Saint Judas*, Wright's style has changed almost completely. The grim formalist had become a kind of mystic realist, looking for—and finding—the transcendent wherever he happened to be—he would apply the same kind of feeling to Italian travels in his late poems. As the decade turned, Wright went from being a tightly enclosed poet of the 1950s to being one of the forerunners of the free and open poetry that would help define the next two decades of writing.

Brenda Hillman

Brenda Hillman, who received her MFA from the Iowa Writers' Workshop in 1976, began as a dark, severe poet who was nonetheless interested in and hopeful about the experiences the world might present to her poems. Like a less-grave Louise Glück's, Hillman's world is booby-trapped, though when the traps are sprung, there are, as often as insights gained at the cost of great pain, wonders to be found.

These lines, from "Aubade," the first poem in Hillman's debut, *White Dress*, would be at home in an early book by Glück:

> One morning you wake and it's gone from you.
> Fear, the daily inheritance,
> The blankness drawing you tenderly up.
> Everything around the bed is left alone,
> So you are quite powerful, and do not move

Here Hillman addresses herself, or a consciousness very near to herself, to whose inner life she has unprecedented access. She tackles a huge subject head-on: fear. And she uses many of Glück's preferred syntactical and tonal techniques: the second-person address to speak to the self ("it's gone from you"); simple, speech-like delivery of broad metaphysical concepts ("Fear, the daily inheritance, / The blankness . . ."); and sudden, short, staccato clauses to ratchet up the poem's tension, creating a sense of the urgency of the inner life ("and do not move"). Hillman doubtlessly got off to a strong start—her early poems are riveting—though not necessarily an original one. The voice of her early poems isn't distinctively hers.

By the middle of her second book, *Fortress*, one has the sense that Hillman is straining for new effects and that, like Plath, she is stronger on technique than on subject matter. A long poem about an ambivalent trip through Walt Disney World finds Hillman observing a family who "helped the old man into the long blue boat / beneath the spires, the topiary gardens; / then, as if part of a burial routine, // the relatives got into the boat beside him / and entered the arch that was dark with singing." There's plenty of great poetry in *Fortress*, but, like Plath in "Sow," Hillman seems to be looking too closely at subjects that lack interest, applying her intensity and technique where, perhaps, it's not needed, where life can't equal it. Would we lose much if we were simply told the family boarded a water ride and took off in it?

Hillman's development parallels that of many 1980s poets, especially her female contemporaries Jorie Graham, C. D. Wright, Lucie Brock-Broido, and Heather McHugh, whose work the poet and critic Stephanie Burt notably termed "elliptical": "Elliptical poets try to manifest a person—who speaks the poem and reflects the poet—while using all the verbal gizmos developed over the last few decades to undermine the coherence of speaking selves." There's a great deal more to it than that, but, to put it simply, Hillman, over the course of the 1980s and early 1990s, proceeded to complicate her poems considerably, including things that strain any definition of the term "verbal gizmos."

Before she got to those "gizmos" in her books of the late 1990s and the first decades of this century, Hillman was in search of subjects and technical apparatus equal to her deep metaphysical curiosity. It took what amounted to a religious conversion to find it, a conversion undergone in response to intense life events—new motherhood, divorce, new love, and the death of a dear friend, among others. Hillman's third and fourth books, *Death Tractates* and *Bright Existence*, which were written together, are almost the work of a wholly new writer. These books take as their inspiration Gnostic religious texts written around the time of Christ. The poems converse with the ideas in these texts, from which they also quote, so that Hillman's early intensity and careful deployment of language have, in this new work, found their purpose and feel attuned to the subjects at hand.

I've been relating Hillman's work to Glück's, because Glück strikes me as the most obvious aesthetic model for her early poems. But in various interviews, Hillman herself cites a far wider circle of early influences that didn't show so obviously in her early poetry. At Iowa, she read deeply in "poetry of linguistic clarity with an expressive emotional range," as she told Phoebe Reeves in an interview, including James Wright and Weldon Kees, as well as Wallace Stevens and John Ashbery. Elsewhere, she talks about Edna St. Vincent Millay, Emily Dickinson, the Bible, and midcentury West Coast avant-gardists Robert Duncan and Denise Levertov, the latter of whom also came to write deeply about social justice movements in her poetry, as Hillman does now. All of this suggests how it often takes time—and a lot of reading and writing—for a poet to manifest in her own work evidence of the voices she is reading and striving to converse with.

In an interview with Patricia Kirkpatrick and Emily August, Hillman explains how she found her way toward the Gnostic texts that would change her poetry: "I first ran across Gnosticism in college. 'Gnostic' as an adjective refers to the sort of anti-cosmic strain of Christian thought that applied to some of the Romantic poets, particularly Blake and Yeats. I put the word on hold for years, and then when Bob [her second husband, the poet Robert Hass] and I started going out, we went vegetable shopping and I said something about loving the shapes of the bell peppers, how they get in these agonized shapes and twist around themselves. Bob answered with some version of 'Bless your little Gnostic heart.' He suggested I read a book by Hans Jonas called *The Gnostic Religion*. Hans Jonas was a scholar of early Gnostic thought who was working without the benefit of the Nag Hammadi texts which were discovered by . . . a shepherd, Mohammed Ali in Egypt." Hillman cites both Jonas and the Nag Hammadi texts as sources in the notes to her two breakthrough books; the Gnostic texts worked for Hillman like translation did for Wright. All of Hillman's subsequent poems have been written, in a sense, in the light cast by her two books based on Gnostic sources.

The transition that takes place in *Death Tractates* and *Bright Existence* is not just from a traditional to an experimental way of writing, but, more deeply, a change from one spiritual viewpoint to another. The early poems view the world like Glück views it, as, essentially, a projection of the viewer's emotions. Gnosticism allowed Hillman to complicate this view. Gnostic beliefs, which are often thought of in a Christian context, are many and complex, drawing together aspects of pagan and monotheistic religions. Gnosticism allowed her to imagine a more permeable relationship between the inner and experiential lives. Through writing her Gnostic poems, she was able to conceive of the evolution of the human inner life as related to the nonhuman world, ultimately to the environment, which, in effect, led Hillman to the ecopoetics of her elemental quartet, the sequence of four books beginning with *Cascadia*.

In "Old Ice" from *Bright Existence* she writes, "Once it seemed the function of poetry / was to redeem our lives. / But it was not. It was to become / indistinguishable from them." This is one of those ars poetica moments, in which a poet states her poetic purpose. It's as if she's describing a poem like "Aubade" from *White Dress*, which takes uncomfortable emotion and recasts it as insight. She's done with that; now, she wants poems to create experiences, "to become / indistinguishable from" life itself.

And this new direction also enabled Hillman to respond to her new life circumstances. As she told Kirkpatrick and August, "When I was newly divorced, which was also a time when the straight-on, simple sentences stopped sounding inside me, it seemed interesting to think about the soul as a process and not just a thing. As Jonas suggests, these are ancient principles from pre-Platonic times—useful really for being in the world with a sense of hope: the soul is on a journey, and the work of being is to evolve."

Here is Hillman's version of childbirth through a Gnostic lens, in a poem called "First Thought":

The moment my daughter was lifted
from me, that sticky
flesh screamed fury,
for she, too, blamed the female body—
I loved it that she screamed—

and I knew I had been sent to earth to understand that pain.

The nurses moved about, doing something
over to the left. Probably weighing her
on what looked like blue tin. The flash of non-
existence always at the edge of vision,
and in the next moment, some unasked-for radiance.

Childbirth is notoriously difficult to write about—not least because the mother is usually disoriented as it's happening ("The nurses moved about, doing something / over to the left. Probably . . .") and because the experience is so powerfully personal. But Hillman's readings in Gnosticism gave her language and context for extraordinary lines like "I knew I had been sent to earth to understand that pain." It's a new sense of purpose she finds: reading her own experience, her newborn's experience, through her reading. Plath's hospital poems—"Tulips," most notably—are about disengagement, distancing the self from experience: "I have given my name and my day-clothes up to the nurses / And my history to the anesthetist and my body to surgeons." Hillman's is about engagement and understanding, a pursuit of the truth of the self and of experience, of the why and how of what happens. This is an esoteric pursuit, and there is of course no one answer nor goal, but if, for Plath, breaking out of constraints required chasing a kind of derangement, Hillman's deepening begs for a spiritual system that allows her to directly ask metaphysical questions. Wright could have written some of these lines. How like the conclusion of "A Blessing" this is:

> then you knew for the bird as for you the world
> split open was stunningly beautiful
> though being alive was nearly impossible—

Hillman could almost "break / Into blossom," and indeed her poem is called "Blossoms Appearing."

Through her Gnostic apprenticeship, Hillman becomes the metaphysical poet she was striving to be, and also begins to think deeply about the relationship between the realms of imagination and of experience, one of Gnosticism's important areas of questioning. The other book to come out of this exploration, *Death Tractates*, tackles personal grief through the same Gnostic lens. Later on, Hillman would take this further in her ecopoetics books.

For all three of these poets, developmental surges are equally a product of willfulness and coincidence. Each of them had to be in the right place at the right time—they were lucky to be standing out in the field where lightning struck, or when the horses were grazing. But they also each decided to leave their cozy rooms, to step into a storm. Berryman plodded along, iterating and re-iterating versions of himself until he found the true voice of *The Dream Songs*; disgusted by his own poetry and desperate for a new direction, Wright decided to translate; Hillman dove deep into

Gnosticism and emerged reborn. None of them could have anticipated where they would end up, and yet none of them could have gotten there without willful action, without making choices. A poet's voice must indeed be found; each poet must venture out to find it.

2. MIDDLES

and

MIRRORS

Mirror Portraits

1.

It's been impossible to enter the world as a new poet in the last half century without bearing at least some of the influence of John Ashbery, who died, at age ninety, in September 2017. His style is the sound of Zeitgeist itself, marked by a casual, conversational tone that accommodates extreme erudition; a breathtakingly wide range of reference, encompassing everything from world literature to popular movies and music to random household objects; and, above all, huge associative leaps between subjects within poems. Even as some of Ashbery's references grow dated, the means of associative thinking his poems reveal are timeless. He worked plenty of internet-era lingo into late books; Ashbery may well have been the great poet of "lingo," isolated bits of vocabulary that stand in for swaths of time and the people who fill them. Ashbery, in his panning, glancing manner, managed to get more of those people into his poems than almost any other contemporary poet. He was able to speak to and for people like and unlike himself by sampling overheard voices in the tapestry of language that composes his poetry.

Broadly, and capacious as he was, Ashbery was really two kinds of poets (which may be one more kind than most): a collage artist and a metaphysical philosopher. The first is in evidence almost everywhere in his work. Ashbery's poems always unfold by free association, even when they try to stick to a topic. The philosopher—a lyrical metaphysician, like Wallace Stevens—is heard from amidst the collages, but rarely does he follow his inquiries through to the end. Ashbery's poems exhibited many other predilections and sources: he was an urban poet, a bit Walt Whitman, a bit T. S. Eliot, a lot Frank O'Hara, his close friend and fellow progenitor of the New York school. He was a magpie like Ezra Pound. He was a mourner like Emily Dickinson. At his best, he ran all of these minds and their musics through his wide-open sensibility, giving what they gave like a producer assembling a powerful backup track out of pieces of the songs he knows and loves.

But Ashbery was a rare poet in another respect—he seemed decidedly unwilling to merge his two strongest strains in most of his poems. In fact, despite a huge body of work, he wrote one particular masterpiece that stands as unique among all his poems, that even might be said to stick out. "Self-Portrait in a Convex Mirror" is his only poem that works as it does—following a strong metaphysical investigation from beginning to end, narrative in its progress through its thinking, long but organized—and perhaps the only great contemporary poem like it that is as good as it is. While he has other extended works—*Three Poems*, "A Wave," *Flow Chart*—none of them has the intense focus of "Self-Portrait," which, unlike the others, does not succumb to extended stretches of wayward association, to mere accretion of material, to a great degree of randomness, though the mind's waywardness and endless associations are two of Ashbery's primary subjects.

More than many other poets, Ashbery fell prey to self-imitation. His allegiance to his own style *is* the limitation of that style. But in "Self-Portrait" he breaks his own rules. It may have taken him his whole writing life until then to establish and perfect those rules and practices, but, on the other side of "Self-Portrait," he was not a new poet; it's as if that poem overtook its author and left him behind when it ended.

The process by which he got there is nothing short of incredible, deserving of Ashbery's worldwide influence. *Some Trees*, chosen by Auden for the Yale Series of Younger Poets, recalled from the rejects when Auden felt he had no other suitable manuscripts in his finalist pile, opens with a startling announcement of a new style:

> We see us as we truly behave:
> From every corner comes a distinctive offering.
> The train comes bearing joy;
> The sparks it strikes illuminate the table.
> Destiny guides the water-pilot, and it is destiny.

In the first line, Ashbery invokes what will become one of his trademarks: a universal "we" to which any reader of his poems suddenly belongs, though the reader hardly feels referred to in particular. Also in that first line is one of Ashbery's signature inversions and deepenings of a cliché—"we" are made visible not as we are, but "as we . . . behave," privileging action over appearance, a surprising virtue for a language artist so obsessed with his material: words. Then comes Ashbery's typically broad invocation of the world, his image of which is "every corner," as though the totality is the sum of otherwise invisible details that remain nonetheless invisible in their naming. The exceptional detail is the vague "distinctive offering"—what are we to make of that? What are we to see behind those words? Whatever we want, whatever we'd care to put there—Ashbery leaves us to supply the answers to his metaphysical questions, including us in the poem while keeping us out, a reminder that words are only made meaningful by their users. "Destiny guides the water-pilot"—what water-pilot? Huh?—he continues, "and it is destiny." This is not wisdom poetry, this poem proclaims; it is an act of mirroring: we are meant to see our own minds in this poem, our own vocabulary. Here is the debut of Ashbery the clever collage artist.

In the title poem of the same book, we meet the philosopher, the classical lyricist, the metaphysician:

> These are amazing: each
> Joining a neighbor, as though speech
> Were a still performance.
> Arranging by chance
>
> To meet as far this morning
> From the world as agreeing
> With it, you and I
> Are suddenly what the trees try
>
> To tell us we are:
> That their merely being there
> Means something; that soon
> We may touch, love, explain.

"Some Trees" foreshadows "Self-Portrait," at least in retrospect, in its odd inquiry into the nature of perception and into how close two people can hope to come to one another. "These" has a clear referent: the trees before Ashbery's eyes. This is not the world "from every corner," but a particular corner, though one shaded vaguely enough that we are allowed to supply our own trees—palm trees for some, maples for others. Then there is that phenomenal thinker of a phrase—"Arranging by chance // To meet as far this morning / From the world as agreeing / With it"—which is as opaque and rewarding as Sylvia Plath's "cloud that distills a mirror to reflect its own slow / Effacement at the wind's hand" in "Morning Song," and as rich. What might it mean? That to agree with the world is to understand the distance the mind creates between the observer and what is observed, that vocabulary is both the bridge and the uncrossable river? This insight leads to the idea that "merely being there / Means something": that to stand before something real is to face the truth of one's distance from people and things, to believe in the possibility that one might "touch, love, explain," and to acknowledge the limits of one's tools—again, words. There's nothing random about this line of thought: it's an inquiry, if an odd one, that arrives at a conclusion, that "Our days put on such reticence / These accents seem their own defense."

Ashbery proceeds in these two manners through the 1950s, '60s, and '70s, trying on different hats and strategies, from formal experiments such as the sestina "The Painter" to the use of found poetry in *The Tennis Court Oath* to the programmatic and generative tactics such as the inclusion of a river in every line of "Into the Dusk-Charged Air." His early development is a survey of avant-garde techniques. *Three Poems*, an exhaustive meditation in prose, is a high point. But Ashbery's 1975 collection *Self-Portrait in a Convex Mirror* is his next major turn, his career's turning point.

But even within that book, the title poem is a serious outlier. Even the opening lyric of the collection, "As One Put Drunk into the Packet-Boat," one of the strongest examples of Ashbery's typical style, is exactly that: typical of Ashbery, though one of the last instances when that style feels truly novel and surprising:

> I tried each thing, only some were immortal and free.
> Elsewhere we are as sitting in a place where sunlight
> Filters down, a little at a time,
> Waiting for someone to come. Harsh words are spoken,
> As the sun yellows the green of the maple tree. . . .

So this was all, but obscurely
I felt the stirrings of new breath in the pages
Which all winter long had smelled like an old catalogue.
New sentences were starting up. But the summer
Was well along, not yet past the mid-point
But full and dark with the promise of that fullness,
That time when one can no longer wander away
And even the least attentive fall silent
To watch the thing that is prepared to happen.

The opening line is *so* good, a moment of profound classical lyricism, a truism that feels true despite the vagueness of "each thing" tried. And there is indeed "new breath in the pages" of this book, but it comes at the end, in the long title poem, which nonetheless invigorates the short poems that precede it. *Can* one write a whole book as good and original as the poem "Self-Portrait in a Convex Mirror"? The title poem seems to come from a seizure of inspiration.

"Self-Portrait" is a different order of poem, on a par with Stevens's great, extended inquiring long works, like "The Comedian as the Letter C" and "Owl's Clover." It's an investigation and an argument, a work of poetic art criticism (Ashbery once paid his bills working as a critic of visual art), and an overwhelming experience of art in itself, a metaphor for and an enacting of what it describes. Ashbery sits before a remarkable piece of art, a self-portrait by the painter Parmigianino, who copied what he saw in a convex mirror on a round ball of wood of the same size. In it, Ashbery finds an inexhaustible representation of what art can hope—and mostly fails—to do: bridge the gap between people living and dead, between distance and time, between what is perceived and what is imagined. It is one of the great poems of our time and Ashbery's most important work.

The poem proceeds by looking, describing, and following the drifts of Ashbery's mind as he is reminded of his own past, his knowledge about this and other artworks (he frequently references a book by Vasari about the painting), and ideas Parmigianino's portrait brings to light. Ashbery's fascination begins with Parmigianino's hand as depicted in the painting, resting in front of the painter's face, "the right hand / Bigger than the head, thrust at the viewer / And swerving easily away, as though to protect / What it advertises." This is one of Ashbery's great phrases, another example of art including us by keeping us out. The hand, distorted, tipped toward the viewer in the reflection and then copied in the painting—which, because it's actually three-dimensional, is something more than a painting—suggests to Ashbery the possibility that what is depicted could actually come out of the depiction, could come nearer to the viewer than merely "flat" art. Of this vexing image, he says, "The soul"—which I take to mean that part of the self that straddles art, the ideal, and life—"establishes itself." "But," the poem goes on to ask—and this is its central question, the one it goes quite a ways toward answering—"how far can it swim out through the eyes / And still return safely to its nest?" Can we actually bridge those gaps between imagination and experience? Ashbery wonders. Can a work of art that is made to actually approach the reader in real space bring us closer to what art depicts: the imagination? And can a poem in which the "you"—"you could be fooled for a moment / Before you realize the reflection/ Isn't yours"—actually means *us*, the readers sitting at the moment of reading before the open book in which the poem is printed, bring us closer to the author's inaccessible inner world, to his perceptions and interpretations, to his very self, "Since it is a metaphor / Made to include us, we are a part of it and / Can live in it as in fact we have done, / Only leaving our minds bare for questioning"?

My purpose here is not to interpret the poem but to describe how it affirms and in some ways defies Ashbery's style. As I have said, the poem works through its argument thoroughly, essayistically. Its point—to prove, for Ashbery through the experience of looking at this work of art and for us through reading this poem, that time is ungraspable, perception unverifiable, but nearly verifiable, through great art—is made using Ashbery's signature style: his leaping thoughts that nonetheless come back to Parmigianino's portrait are the evidence. The mind, the self, the poem indicates, is subject to uncontrollable randomness, to its own memories and to what the body senses, but it orbits a somewhat stable self—"the whole is stable within / Instability," Ashbery writes. Elsewhere in his poetry, instability merely functions to prove its own insistence, but here it illustrates something we have in common; free association is not really so free, returning again and again to the same self and its thoughts and perceptions, and to the painting.

"Self-Portrait" is stuffed with portable maxims, aphorisms, mini-essays, that could be plucked from the poem as Ashbery's phrases often can, but here also argue toward the poem's point: "the soul is not a soul, / Has no secret, is small, and it fits / Its hollow perfectly: its room, our moment of attention"; "your eyes proclaim / That everything is surface. The surface is what's there / And nothing can exist except what's there"; "Tomorrow is easy, but today is uncharted." Ashbery's humor, when it comes up—this may be Ashbery's most serious poem, too—is anything but flippant: his wit makes metaphors that support his case, like "a dozing whale on the sea bottom / In relation to the tiny, self-important ship / On the surface." His wit here isn't parsable from his seriousness; it's one of its expressions.

It's as if a different poet wrote "Self-Portrait," or the same poet had used all his previous poems as practice for this one, though subsequent poems don't always utilize the imaginative energy this one generates. Take a few examples, picked almost at random, from

three different collections from two different decades. In them, we
see Ashbery's late style, basically his style after "Self-Portrait":

> But such storms exude strange
> resonance: The power of the Almighty
> reduced to its infinitesimal root
> hangs like the chant of bees . . .
> > *"Still Life with Stranger" from* Hotel Lautréamont *(1992)*

> And in a little while we broke under the strain:
> suppurations ad nauseam, the wanting to be taller,
> though it's simply about being mysterious, i.e., not taller,
> like any tree in any forest.
> > Mute, the pancake describes you.
> It had tiny Roman numerals embedded in its rim.
> > *"Chinese Whispers" from* Chinese Whispers *(2002)*

> Try to avoid the pattern that has been avoided,
> the avoidance pattern. It's not as easy as it looks:
> The herringbone is floating eagerly up
> from the herring to become parquet. Or whatever suits it.
> New fractals clamor to be identical
> to their sisters. Half of them succeed.
> > *"Sonnet: More of Same" from* Where Shall I Wander *(2005)*

It's easy to perform the same kind of close readings of the associative material in these lines: one is tempted to linger over "the chant
of bees," to beg one's inner senses to hear the sound, which must be
beautiful, though there is nothing in it as rich as anything in "Some
Trees." Ashbery has certainly grown sillier as he's progressed—
"Mute, the pancake describes you." Perhaps the suggestion that we
"avoid the pattern that has been avoided, / the avoidance pattern"

is taking flippancy too far—one feels that this is vocabulary deployed for its own sake, a kind of weighted nonsense the intent of which is to prove the futility of paraphrase. I can't get too excited about any of these as individual poems, single works meant to have the weight of complete pieces of literature. As examples of a style, they do their job: if I wanted "More of Same"—a revealing title if ever there was one—late Ashbery is where I'd look.

Which is not to condemn Ashbery's last three decades of writing. He has a point—many points—to make: while vocabulary changes over time, its utility and its limitations stay about the same. But if that *is* the point, it flies in the face of what many of us hope poetry can accomplish: the construction of a bridge—albeit a flimsy one—between inner and outer worlds. And when one is in the mood for Ashbery, *this* Ashbery, there is no one else. Except of course his throngs of younger imitators, many of whom have made their master's late techniques do a good deal more work, keeping more balls in the air, than their originator.

My point, for now, in the preceding examples is to show that, somewhere after the 1980s, Ashbery seems to have ceased to be very interested in what *else* his poems might accomplish; he was mostly content to reiterate them. There is not much more development. The strategies haven't changed or advanced. This is hardly an unusual eventuality for a poet, and lesser poets have, perhaps, only one thing to say, one aesthetic ax to grind in their whole careers. "Self-Portrait in a Convex Mirror" is enough poetry to justify a whole career; Ashbery's body of work justifies at least two.

2.

Susan Wheeler's body of work may be the best compliment John Ashbery could ever receive. While Ashbery's style and concerns have been aped to some extent by perhaps half the poets to come along in the last quarter century, no one but Wheeler has actually tried as hard, nor succeeded, through the creation of her own art, to understand, by imitation then extension, Ashbery's particular mind, as if from the inside. Something in Wheeler wants to *be* Ashbery, at least to think some of his thoughts; or, perhaps more precisely, by wearing an Ashbery costume, Wheeler has been able to come closer to herself, her own quirky, polyphonic, polylingual voice that, like Ashbery's, moves through the histories and registers of the English language and its linguistic cousins as if in search of, though without real hope of finding, the meanings those languages orbit. Plus, to those high-minded concerns of Ashbery's Wheeler adds a sexiness and wariness of the language used to discuss sex, and a more pointed interrogation of the ways so many of our problems—especially in terms of money and power—are *in* the language, rather than simply expressed by it. These are the subjects of Wheeler's major long poem and her most self-conscious tribute to Ashbery's "Self-Portrait," "The Debtor in the Convex Mirror."

Wheeler's early poems, while fun, funny, whimsical, and interesting, are not, in light of Wheeler's increasingly significant and individual later work, imperative reading, except inasmuch as they introduce her predilections, point to her later work, and narrate her apprenticeship to Ashbery. In them, we meet a poet as drawn to following as to breaking formal rules—there are plenty of sonnets, careful rhyme schemes, carefully chosen and percussive words, and there are as many poems that spill irregularly down the page and sound relaxed if not prosy. These poems also exhibit a then-new poet who has intensely studied Ashbery and the other major New York school writers, plus all the poets they read, and run their ideas through her own sensibility thirty years after they first published. As in the poems of her forebears, varied voices and dictions flow together, almost without regard for the divisions between high, low, new, and old registers. A couplet like this one, which concludes the poem "Bag 'O' Diamonds," is a good example: "Oh yet who considereth the faith / Can ye slam the wong straight?"

And, like any good new poet, she tells us in one early poem—if not, obliquely, in all of them—how to read her:

> . . . it is this voice that makes you
> swoon: this story is one loosening tool listing into another,
> each bearing its affects like wants, like tricksters' cups.
> Sleep now: it is always in the telling, not the tale.

In this early instance, Wheeler signals that we need not be as concerned with the subject as much as the matter—the materials—of her poems. This is one of the basic tenets of Ashbery's style, but Wheeler gives it her own particular, and peculiar, flair. Note the use of the archaic "tricksters' cups" and invocation of fairy tales in the last line. Wheeler is endlessly fascinated with both the more and less recognizable elements of the linguistic past, perhaps in a more precise way than Ashbery. This seems a good time, too, to underscore one of the most prevalent aspects of Wheeler's poetry: whatever else it is, whomever else she's conjuring when she writes, Wheeler's poems are weird. This poet has a very odd imagination. Wheeler's vision includes everything from fairly ironic, adorable humor (one poem describes "a child come into an awesome puberty"); to brat-pack movie slang ("she had said they were dweebs"); to intensely private, almost interior language reminiscent of Theodore Roethke and, more recently, Mary Jo Bang ("they eat grass in the night, bo, bo"); to perhaps even blackface in one poem that mentions "a special s'rup 't cures the lonelies." Despite the clear admission of her influences throughout the poems—and a writer's particular synthesis of her influences can be a sign of originality, too—perhaps only Wheeler would actually recognize herself in the totality of what's here. What Wheeler has done most significantly is to take Ashbery and co. somewhere they did not go, turning their romanticism and drifting amalgams of language toward a focused, if often hard to summarize, investigation of what makes the contemporary American language expressive of contemporary America.

It's in her third book, *Source Codes*, that Wheeler really gets going, and in her fourth collection, *Ledger*, that she accomplishes something no one has before, bringing all her interests and influences together to make poems that reflect an America no one else has seen (though no one but the very smart and literary, perhaps, has looked for it). In "Produce, Produce," Wheeler sends up Frost's famous "Provide, Provide," trading Frost's comfortingly conclusive, if haunting, aphoristic ending—"Better to go down dignified / With boughten friendship at your side / Than none at all. Provide, provide!"—for a far more disturbing observation about America's tremendous appetite, even for what it's already got:

> If hunger takes them to the coast,
> They find a spectacle to toast.
> Of several of their peers to roast.
>
> Those that make it to the south
> Are lucky to live thumb to mouth.
> They might prefer the Catamount
>
> Where greenish mountains freeze the nuts.
> Though scavenging is an art that's bust
> The ravenous can be beauty sluts.
>
> Those lucky few who adduce
> The food that keeps them from the noose
> Will crave on, too. Produce, produce.

Still quirky and odd ("mountains freeze the nuts"), Wheeler's also hit her stride and found her deeper subject. Hidden in Frost's already dark poem is an even scarier notion of how love in America might work: we never get enough, and since real love can't actually be bought—"boughten friendship" is not friendship—what we need is distraction, busywork, stuff to consume. A perfect moral in our age of constant device upgrades and in-app purchases.

In *Ledger*, that's exactly what we get. Wheeler's most unified book, and the real payoff for getting to know how Wheeler works in the earlier poems, *Ledger* meditates on and exploits the language of commerce and consumer culture. These poems, many of them long, sprawling collages, ask faux-pressing questions, like "who bears the Count Chocula shipment up," and go as far as to simply list the terms of the internet-age poetic economy:

> Tyvek Bruce Willis Buffalo Bertelsmann Turtle Wax Tiger Balm
> Nickel Cadmium Postgraduate Ice Cube Waldrop
> Exile Witness Nike Iowa Snapple Foucault, The Sands
> Browning Tradition, Hejinian, Bly—SKU, ADP, BAP
> Time-Warner, Ted Turner, The Favorite Poem Project, the Oulipo,
>   the Fed
> Independent Cinema, Mrs. B's, Miss Lou, Reds

While this was written a few years before the Great Recession, this is the poetry of America's post-9/11 economic downturn. Among other things, passages like this acknowledge, with some bitterness, that even poetry is commodified. But this is not mere cynicism: Wheeler finds it wonderful, too, that in our time these disparate terms can hang together and make meaning of their own. If an SKU (the code assigned to each product a store sells) is equated with BAP (the annual *Best American Poetry* anthologies), then, too, perhaps the poetry Ph.D. program at SUNY Buffalo does something, however small, to nullify some of the commodification of art committed by Bertelsmann (the conglomerate that owned Random House before it merged with Penguin to become the world's behemoth publisher).

Wheeler's biggest and best poem is her fifteen-page "The Debtor in the Convex Mirror," a major work of the new millennium. The title, of course, is a riff on Ashbery's. Wheeler's title refers to yet another painting, *The Money Changer and His Wife*, by sixteenth-century Flemish painter Quentin Massys, which depicts the eponymous couple and, reflected in a convex mirror on a table, a man in a red cap sitting where the viewer would be. Quite a bundle of meta—a poem about a painting and about a poem that is itself about another painting, all of which is rolled up into an ambitious meditation on what it is to give and to owe.

"The Debtor in the Convex Mirror" is addressed to Ashbery and quotes "Self-Portrait" occasionally. She says to Ashbery, acknowledging him as a kind of master (the italics are Wheeler's quotation from "Self-Portrait"): "*My guide in these matters is your self,* // your own soul permeable by beauty,   and mine not, / not even by the swirling of facts." She comes right out and says she's after Ashbery's vision, which she takes far too seriously to merely imitate. The Ashbery she wants to understand and follow is the metaphysical one who asks (again, quoting "Self-Portrait"), "how far, indeed, // can the soul *swim out through the eyes and still return safely to its nest?*"). Then she performs the same kind of poetic transposition of the Massys painting as Ashbery does of the Parmigianino: "we see, we viewers, / sitting right where we are, a red-hatted man who holds // a book to his chin as though he is sunning. Rather, / he's reading—or trying." And so, we, the readers of Wheeler's poem, become the man in the Massys painting, which is inside Wheeler's poem, which is itself an attempt to get inside Ashbery's poem. Wheeler's poem reaches its climax in a passage in the middle:

The painter in the mirror wants privacy, not this call that invades
the reading of a book. Your own looked out at us, but mine, *Massys*—
disingenuous, masquerading, stressed and damp—doesn't; weightier
things on his mind he's got not. But he only pretends to absorption.
It's we who discern the privacy he wants, we who can see
what he lacks. It's as though we're instructed to trust the lender,
his own fix being more, well, *sequestered*.
The last century mined focus as a notion, and even here in Manhattan,
a delirium of sorts swabbing its streets,
we tread with the intensity of hounds,
plugged into our earpiece conjointments, or collecting loose change
off of cuffs. Massys' grimace underdramatizes our lot.

In the painting Wheeler has chosen, we must assume it's the debtor,
Massys, the painter, who's reflected in the mirror ball on the banker's
desk. As in Ashbery's poem, it's a self-portrait, but in the preceding
passage, Wheeler notes the difference between Ashbery's self-portrait
and hers, which is also the difference between their two poetic
visions, and the distance Wheeler has been able to push Ashbery's
aesthetic ideas. "Your own looked out at us," Wheeler says to
Ashbery of his subject, Parmigianino, and it's true: Parmigianino
faces us, his eyes looking directly at the viewer, offering a mysterious invitation—he wants us to look into his magic re-creation of a
mirror and think, for a moment, that we're him. Massys, however,
depicts himself as "disingenuous, masquerading, stressed and damp."
Sitting across from the banker, from whom he is likely taking out
a loan, Massys simply wants the transaction over with; he wants
to be alone. It's as if the self-portrait is not directed at the audience
at all, though only we, who are the transaction's outside observers,
"discern the privacy he wants, we who can see / what he lacks."

What he lacks, so Wheeler contends, is what all of us in contemporary America, with its "delirium of sorts swabbing its streets,"

can't get enough of: respite from the barrage of information in which we're all drowning, whether we're in public or by ourselves. For Wheeler, "The soul *negotiates* its right of way" out of the eyes, "but not without a bargain struck *without*." To be in the world, even to use the world's words, you must give up yourself; hence the Massys painting becomes for Wheeler a metaphor for the kinds of transactions we are constantly engaging in: between lender and borrower, writer and reader, self and other. To get something, something else must be given in exchange: which is why, later in the poem, Wheeler calls Massys a "bad risk." He wants out of the whole stream of correspondences. Though of course he really doesn't—he wants to communicate his complex ambivalence about communication, or else why paint himself in? The same ambivalence energizes Wheeler's poem.

Taken together, what Ashbery and Wheeler show us is that poetic development does not begin and end with one poet's career. Where Ashbery drops one thread at the end of "Self-Portrait," with its "whispers out of time," Wheeler picks it up and carries the argument—by way of the philosophical, free-associating, questioning style—into a new era in which Ashbery's mind is less at home. At one deep level, both poets are after—in both the senses of pursuit and imitation—those things that have fallen between the cracks in the words and are lost somewhere in time, barely surviving in the poems as echoes.

Influences Illuminated: francine j. harris

1.

We tend to define poetic influence in terms of how a later poet is shaped by an earlier one. This definition perhaps oversimplifies what poetic influence is: the internalization and adaptation of other poets' work into a new style. Poetry is a reader's art: poets make poems in response to the poems they've read. Poetry is a special way of communicating, through symbols and gestures, insinuations, through fakes and feints. Robert Frost said it "provides the one permissible way of saying one thing and meaning another." It requires like-minded conversation partners, other poets and poems communicating in this way. Poems are strange among linguistic artifacts, not useful in a practical sense. They'd cause confusion, for instance, on street signs; they're art objects, metaphors in themselves, meant to represent the more practical uses of language.

Poems take place in many kinds of conversations, whether with other poems and poets, with an imagined reader, with the culture at large, or with the poet's own previous, current, or future selves. An implicit response follows all lines of poetry. Poetic influence occurs as an aspect of these conversations, a volleying between poets living and dead. The influence of one poet upon another is neither simple nor singular, but a matrix of experiences of other poetry absorbed, adapted, smeared, blended, spat out. All poets have many influences in evidence at various times throughout their work, though hopefully well-enough assimilated that they're not obvious—hopefully a poet's influences have been adapted, changed, and put to new uses.

But let's try an experiment: instead of reading forward, let's read backward, analyzing older poets in terms of newer ones, to see whether a broader constellation of influences can be made visible. After all, it's only in hindsight that we can trace influence at all, by isolating characteristics in a new poet's work that match or might be derived from the work of an old one. No poet simply copies her forebears. Each poet stands at the epicenter of her own set of circumstances—her upbringing, her engagement with various communities, her lifelong exposure to language—meaning her voice is of necessity different from anyone else's. A significant poet will internalize and alchemize the influence of many other poets and press them through her own sensibility, resulting in poems in which it's possible to locate aspects of previous poets' styles, but which are hers alone.

Investigating poetic development presents an intriguing problem: how to discuss and describe the development of very new poets who have not yet published enough poetry to demonstrate much artistic change. What can be seen in new poets' work, however, are the ways poetry itself changes over time, what the art form keeps and discards from its passing practitioners, how poetry itself develops through the work of many poets over many decades.

2.

I'm going to take a close look at the work of one extraordinary new poet, francine j. harris (like ee cummings, she writes her name in lowercase when it's associated with her poetry), whose highly original poems—published so far in two books, *allegiance* (2012) and *play dead* (2016)—demonstrate a wide range of influences absorbed and put to new uses or old uses in new contexts.

Harris is a black woman whose upbringing and adult residence in the city of Detroit are major subjects for her poetry. So are the subtle and overt manifestations of racism, especially against blacks, in America. She is also a formal and verbal innovator, bringing together elements of the experimental and modernist traditions in American poetry with aspects of performance poetry and the confessional lyric. From all of these strains, it's easy to draw lines backward to harris's forerunners, but it's also startling to see how, by combining them, she's created powerful new poetry for our time.

In many ways, harris—who also chooses not to capitalize the pronoun "I," and ignores a number of other conventions of grammar and style—is a model contemporary poet. If contemporary poetry has a hallmark, it is variety: the best poets of this period are neither experimental nor traditional, neither formal nor free, neither political nor aesthete. They are all of these things at once, blending styles and modes. This could be said of previous poets as well, but never before have poets been so encouraged to claim many schools, to be many kinds of poet. A formalist, a confessional poet, a protest poet, a love poet, and more, harris is a skeptic about the possibilities of language to affect change and create bridges between individuals. Her best poems demonstrate the breadth of what a contemporary poem can be, making her an ideal case study in how the work of older poets, and contemporaries, is exerting influence on new poetry.

I'm going to elucidate a number of the stylistic mannerisms that harris seems to have adapted from other poets. I don't know whether she has in fact read all, or any, of them, or whether she is aware of their influence on her work. But the indications of influence are rarely as linear and obvious as Susan Wheeler's adaptation of John Ashbery's "Self-Portrait in a Convex Mirror" in her "The Debtor in the Convex Mirror." Sometimes, it's only in the work of the newer poet that we can identify the achievements of the older ones. The marks of a wide array of poets, from cummings to

Robert Hayden to Lucille Clifton to D. A. Powell, appear in harris's work. And there are plenty of others in the mix as well.

3.

Let me start with an obvious influence. I can't imagine francine j. harris hasn't read Clifton deeply and at length. By the time harris must have been starting her serious poetic pursuits in the 1990s, Clifton was one of America's most acclaimed poets. The hallmarks of her style—extreme concision, seemingly simple language that conceals layered meanings, broad historical reference, timeless authority, and an alignment with various streams of twentieth-century protest poetry—were widely imitated, and are present in some form in harris's own distinctive poems. The two poets share elements of a literary mission: to fashion a highly personal and individual voice that can nonetheless engage the larger community of African Americans. And they both write out of urban landscapes, transposing the pastoral mode to the city. Both of them seem to subscribe deeply to the school of poetic thought that stresses the inseparability of the personal and the political. Clifton would have been a necessary and liberating model, a jumping-off point for harris.

The first poem in 1969's *good times*, Clifton's first published collection, is called "in the inner city." It's the kind of ars poetica that signals a new poet's new voice. Here it is in its entirety:

in the inner city
or
like we call it
home
we think a lot about uptown
and the silent nights
and the houses straight as

dead men
and the pastel lights
and we hang on to our no place
happy to be alive
and in the inner city
or
like we call it
home

As usual with Clifton's work, this is a seemingly simple poem with deep undertones. Clifton is a poet of icons, broad strokes that are meant to indicate a vast swath of specifics. The fanciest word here is "pastel," and it's pretty accessible. In the poem's first phrase, "in the inner city / or / like we call it / home," Clifton makes a number of claims. The first line signals the pastoral, the communing with one's environment. To outsiders—white readers, perhaps, "uptown"—"inner city" indicates a kind of forbidden zone, a frightening place where they won't be welcome. But right away, Clifton makes it clear that this poem is not spoken by an outsider—it is uttered on behalf of a collective, a "we" for whom the "inner city" is "home." When Clifton repeats that phrase at the poem's conclusion, after shading in the aspects of this "no place" that frighten even the insiders—"the houses straight as / dead men"—as well as its beauty, such as the "pastel lights," the repetition indicates resignation as well as celebration. This is Clifton wringing deep meaning out of a seemingly simple poem, as if to indicate the unjust circumstances African Americans are forced to live with, as well as their capacity to fashion a "home" despite those circumstances. So "in the inner city" is a protest poem as much as a pastoral, railing subtly against subjugation and imprisonment in the city, but also claiming the deep and personal dignity that makes this community "happy to be alive."

Her take on this theme, perhaps her version of this poem, called "i live in detroit," which appears early in harris's first book, is far longer and more specific, but uses many of the same techniques. It's a ghazal, a classical form with roots in Iranian, Indian, and Pakistani music, but which was popularized among modern American poets by Agha Shahid Ali, the revered Kashmiri American poet who lived and published in the United States from the 1970s until his death in 2001. A popular poet and an influential teacher of poetry, Ali's own ghazals and his advocacy of the form in anthologies and classes made the ghazal into a staple for American poets from the 1980s onward—seemingly everyone wrote a few.

The ghazal, as it's practiced here, is a series of somewhat independent couplets that share a typically melancholy theme and use a repeated word or phrase at the end of the last line of each couplet. For harris, that phrase is "in detroit," and the poem serves as a sad ode to her hometown, illuminating its beauty and its darkness in much the same way Clifton's poem does for her archetypal "inner city." Here's a part of it:

> she said i live in detroit. and there are no flowers in detroit.
> so why would anyone in detroit write about flowers in detroit.
>
> i don't tell her we live under the trees. root up curbs and dam fire
>   hydrants
> to water black pansies licked to the sides of popped black balloons
>   in detroit.
> . . . .
> there are plenty of violets in flophouses. pistils broken open
> on forty-ounce mouth lids making honeybees bastards in detroit.
>
> i don't tell her look around you. i don't point out the bottoms of
>   coffee cups

> where the city spits iris and scratches the back of your throat in
> detroit.

An expansive poet, harris is also an extemporizer. Many of her
poems, though not this one, stretch a few pages and feel splashed
across the canvas, as though improvised; close examination shows
she is in complete control. Like Clifton, harris is a poet of icons and
subtle undercurrents in her lines, but she is a poet of the internet
age, so she has a lot more language to compete and contend with.
Clifton, writing at the end of the 1960s, a time of protests and accessible, loud slogans, the energy of which she tried to incorporate
into her poems, could get what she wanted out of broad strokes.
One feels that harris, spurred by endless, anxious social media
feeds, wants to get everything into her lines. Hence her poems are
often overwhelmed and overwhelming.

But this one, due to its form, feels fairly tidy and controlled.
Flowers are harris's version of Clifton's "pastel lights." "There are
no flowers in detroit. / so why would anyone in detroit write about
flowers in detroit," the poem's interlocutor asks. In responding,
harris also claims a collective community—"we live under the
trees"—and the poem works, with subtle anger and celebration, to
show the outsider why "we are happy to be alive" "in detroit" and
offer the insider a sense of familiarity and kinship.

This poet, too, has her "inner city" to explain. There are flowers
in Detroit, harris asserts, both the plants and the people who have
grown strong in spite of dark circumstances. The power of plants to
split pavement—like William Carlos Williams's "flower that splits /
the rocks"—is the poem's central metaphor. Despite the lack of
lush greenery, the people of inner-city Detroit "root up curbs and
dam fire hydrants / to water black pansies," a figure for black children playing in the spray of opened hydrants.

Where Clifton could make do with the iconic "pastel lights," harris chooses to specify, taking us through a cascade of layered metaphors, flowers that are people blooming despite adversity. And all her images are double-edged, simultaneously grim and hopeful, protesting and celebrating at once. "There are plenty of violets in flophouses," she writes, and "some of our mothers rescued begonias with cheap plastic planters," showing these city-dwellers importing natural beauty into their environment, adopting a kind of actual pastoral.

Of course harris is angry: life for inner-city blacks hasn't improved much, and, "like a lot of flowers," these are at the mercy of larger forces: "i have split my stem. cleaved into root balls. stuck to sweaty / bus windows. like so much dandelion, i get rinsed down shelter shower drains in detroit." The poet exhibits a split self, both a victim of centuries of unforgivable treatment that have led to poverty and few opportunities, and also, like Clifton, a celebrant of her community's endurance and strength, claiming her "home."

At the end of the poem, harris finds herself wishing for access to nature and beauty the city simply can't—won't—afford. Her ending—"if I can't leave. is that enough flower grounded in detroit"—renders her flower metaphor highly ironic: these flowers are both "grounded," as in rooted, at home, and ground down, minimized, subjugated. The outsider who, at the poem's beginning, says "there are no flowers in detroit" is schooled by the poem. The poem is meant to warn this person of how much she misunderstands: there are flowers, but not the kind she assumes. To say there are none dismisses Detroit's survival and empowerment; it's an insult.

And reading backward from harris to Clifton adds a shade of irony to Clifton's ending, too, lending the word "home" another layer, forcing outsiders to confront the difference between what they, and the inner-city citizens, call theirs.

4.

Clifton and Ali are only two among many sources traceable in harris's work. Perhaps more influential on her poems is D. A. Powell, who I believe to be the major poet to arise in the 1990s and now among the most important writing. Like harris's, Powell's poems stand at the convergence of many streams; Powell may be, for instance, the only poet to show how the Bible and 1980s club music are of equal value to poetry, if used properly. Powell is an imperative poetic chronicler of HIV and AIDS from the 1980s through today; his language is equally rooted in the time it describes and timeless. Put simply, Powell's work combines both important subject matter and major formal innovation. Many poets do one or the other, but few do both so seamlessly, with such deep roots in the history of language itself.

Powell's most obvious innovation is his long, expansive line. A line is a poem's basic unit, meant to symbolize or visualize a unit of thought, a packet of language that belongs together, according to poet and poem. It's a verbal scene, a view from the poem's window. This notion—one packet to one line—worked for much of the history of poetry, when it was more natural to imagine and musically score thoughts occurring one at a time (though of course they never did). But what's the appropriate line for a time of many thoughts at once, for layers of associations, for vision saturated with media, for an era when the mind is battered with and invites information from all directions? Powell developed and honed his own version of a single line that could accommodate multiple lines in one, many packets.

The gaps in the poems' long lines function a little like semicolons in sentences: the separated phrases are, or could be, lines of their own, but they have too much to do with each other to be separated. They are parts of a single thought, spilling into each other backward and forward across the line, and so can't be separated by a dramatic line break. In this way, Powell gets more than one line into a line, asserting something about how we make associations now. The contemporary, media-saturated mind brings up memories and ideas in slanted relations to one another, reminding one another of each other. Powell began writing before the internet was omnipresent; he wrote out of what might be called the first era of media saturation, since, maybe, the 1950s, and out of a camp sensibility, with pop music, film, TV, literature, and product placement all blurring together. Powell's is a poetry of reminders. Songs recall experiences recall places recall times recall people recall songs, and so on.

A quick glance makes Powell's influence on harris obvious— even from a distance, the poems look similar. Let's take two poems with related themes, the first a possible model for the second. Here is all of Powell's short "[nicholas the ridiculous: you will always be 27 and impossible. no more expectations]":

> nicholas the ridiculous: you will always be 27 and impossible.   no
>   more expectations
> you didn't carry those who went in long cars after you.   stacking
>   lie upon lie as with children
> swearing "no" to pain and "yes" to eternity.   you would have
>   been a bastard: told the truth
>
> afternoons I knelt beside your hiding place   [this is the part
>   where you speak to me from beyond]
> *and he walks with me and he talks with me.   he tells me that I am*
>   *his own.*   dammit
> nothing.   oh sure once in a while a dream.   a half-instant.   but
>   you are no angel you are
>
> repeating the same episodes: nick at night.   tricky nick.   nicholas
>   at halloween a giant tampon

don't make me mature by myself: redundancy of losing common
    ground.   for once be serious

And here is part of harris's longish poem "katherine with the
lazy eye. short. and not a good poet":

this morning, i heard you were found in your mcdonald's uniform.

i heard it while i was visiting a lake town, where empty
woodsy highways turn into waterside drives.

i'd forgotten my toothbrush and was brushing my teeth with one
    finger.
a friend who didn't know you said he'd heard it like this: *you know
    katherine. short.*

with a lazy eye. poet. not a very good one. yeah, well she died. the
    blue on that lake
isn't so frank. it fogs off into the horizon like styrofoam. the

picnic tables full of white people. i ask them where the coffee is.
    they say at meijer.

i wonder if you thought about getting out of detroit. when you
    read at the open mic
you'd point across the street at mcdonald's and tell us to come
    see you.

katherine with the lazy eye. short and not a good poet, i guess
    i almost cried.
i don't know why, because i didn't like you. this is the first
    i remembered your name.

Both poems are elegies for lost community members—nicholas a friend and fellow clubgoer who died of AIDS, and katherine a fellow poet. Nicholas was beloved, katherine disliked. Both leave the poems' speakers feeling guilty, longing for a chance to speak again. Both poems deal with a kind of ambivalent love and a complicated, abstract, distant form of loss.

Again, I can't know if harris read Powell or had this poem in mind, but it seems likely she had taken in his work. Her long line certainly suggests Powell's influence, but it could have come directly or through the many other poets who have imitated Powell. Regardless, reading backward from harris to Powell, the relation between the two poems is undeniable. In both poems, the line is made to contain several thoughts, several packets (though Powell's is more staccato).

The poems' similarities don't stop with the line. Powell's nicholas "will always be 27 and impossible," a young man frozen in time, his youthful mischief and stubbornness preserved by death. Similarly, katherine will always be the young woman "with the lazy eye. short. and not a good poet," an unfulfilled artist for all eternity. These two titular descriptive clauses even unfold in the same way: the physical markers—nicholas's age, katherine's lazy eye and height—then the character traits after the word "and"—"impossible," "not a good poet." Both of these character descriptions are also fears the poems' speakers harbor about themselves, cautionary tales, roads thankfully not taken. Perhaps Powell survived because of his changeability; he was, perhaps, not "impossible." Harris became a good poet, and so was able to transcend her circumstances. And, of course, both went on to become chroniclers of those who, unlike themselves, couldn't survive AIDS and the damnations of Detroit, so that both of these poems enact a kind of survivor's guilt.

Powell developed his expansive poetry to accommodate the high and low—the funerary "long cars," for instance, and the television reruns on "nick at night"—and harris takes this further into the internet age, anxiously including all the details. Katherine is also "impossible," though, as is always the case in harris's extemporaneous poetry, the poem is specific about it: "i didn't like how you followed around a married man," she writes, whereas nicholas is accused more vaguely of "stacking lie upon lie."

The failings of nicholas and katherine are enumerated in both poems. In life and then in death, nicholas fails as a lover: he "*tells me that I am his own.   dammit / nothing.   oh sure once in a while a dream*"; in a later part of her poem, harris describes how katherine let "some homeless dude / flirt with you." Both, through a kind of irresponsibility or desperation, succumb to their environments' hazards, AIDS for nicholas, violence "in an abandoned building" for katherine. Neither could adapt and protect themselves. But, in the poems, each is a projection of the speaker's fear. For Powell, nicholas is a cautionary tale about the dangers of promiscuous sex in an age of disease; "for once be serious" he entreats this man who is "no angel," doomed to "repeating the same episodes" in Powell's memory, offering no new wisdom or advice. For harris, katherine, who foolishly lived "like nothing's gonna get you," can't show the way, in this elegy, "to leave detroit." For both poets, elegy is primarily a forum for grief, for remembering the world that was; whatever wisdom the poems offer is hard to apply, because it applies to the past rather than the present.

What's not hard to apply or identify are the ways these poems converse with one another, and how, reading them together, they inform each other. Beyond the obvious similarities in the poetic line and the elegizing of a community, harris extends Powell's oversaturated gaze, and in so doing, offers a lens through which we can reread Powell—some of harris's expansive urban catalog might fit inside Powell's concise glossing of a troubled decade: it's easy to imagine the lists of places and things, from strobe lights in clubs to hospital beds, that Powell might include. Both poets take a great deal from Whitman, though Powell opts for his shorter prophetic lyrics whereas harris imitates his seemingly endless American catalogs.

Reading harris helps us more deeply read Clifton, Ali, Powell, Whitman, and others. Her work is a sort of fulfillment of theirs, a part of those poets' bids for literary longevity. Their subjects, forms, and styles enabled a new poet to speak. It is in this way that poetry is carried forward.

We read Homer, William Blake, John Keats, and W. B. Yeats because their poems tell us something about the present, because today's poets still find in their poems means to say what they must. But it's through the lenses of today's poetry that we read yesterday's, through the aperture of today's necessities. Poets who only tell the stories of the past do not survive except as artifact. Many other poets beyond Clifton, Ali, and Powell have helped make harris's poems possible—good and great poets assimilate a constellation of influences in ways that are both obvious and undetectable. But poetry is as much an art of reading as it is of writing, and the poetry of the past is an essential element of the atmosphere that enables present poets to breathe and to sing.

A Long Career: W. S. Merwin

1.

Major poets make themselves, with effort; they are not born. I would argue that many major poets begin minor, though the best of them begin with the promise of becoming important voices for their time. They begin weird, out of step in some fundamental way, esoteric, in their own heads. Eventually, their strangeness comes to shape the poetry around them. They give voice to the poetry of their time, and one can no longer understand it without understanding them. W. S. Merwin is such a poet, both strange and essential. He is the poet of his time in part because he shaped the language with which we have described his era in poetry. He helped shape our notion of a contemporary poem, though his style is so much his own that no one has imitated it effectively—except Merwin himself. For he is also an example of another kind of poet: the kind who, like John Ashbery, develops such virtuosity in his voice that he has perfected it and become his own imitator.

Maybe this happens to most poets, though mostly when they're relatively young, not in their seventies and eighties, when it happened for Merwin. Most poets find a voice, a form, a mode, often in their thirties or forties, and continue to issue versions of the same poem for the rest of their lives.

Merwin's development is not like T. S. Eliot's or W. B. Yeats's, both of whom continually found new facets of their styles, and is instead more like Wallace Stevens's. Both Merwin and Stevens attained such a level of virtuosity in his own voice that their late poems can seem to be almost a product of habit—but what extraordinary technique to have in one's muscle memory!

Merwin's life's work in poetry is now available in four books: a two-volume set that includes all his collections through 2008's *The Shadow of Sirius*, and his collections *The Moon Before Morning* and *Garden Time*. The staggering thing about a life's work is that it takes a lifetime to complete. Which is to say having a writer's collected writings means having the chance to attempt to comprehend a life, or a life's summary, in terms of whatever parts of a self make art. Each of a poet's poems was once, if only for a few moments, the absolute forefront of that poet's life, the forward edge of the self, the object of all of the mind's attention. How remarkable, to be able to imagine a whole person's whole gaze. Reading across these books, one senses Merwin's life pressing urgently on his artistic development.

Merwin is unlike any other American poet. His poems are related to those of Ted Hughes (the two were close friends in the 1950s), but Merwin's are more varied. Merwin is a capacious, old-fashioned kind of poet. He is more like the great twentieth-century Polish poets, Czeslaw Milosz and especially Zbigniew Herbert, in terms of the scope of his ambition and the development of his style across his whole career. He's a moralist, a fabulist, a maker of myths skimmed off history. Merwin takes the long view of current events. He is the kind of person one thinks of when one thinks of a poet—wizardly in appearance, deep eyed, off the grid (he lives on a tree preserve of his own cultivation in Haiku, on the island of Maui in Hawaii). The voice that speaks his poems—simultaneously oracular, mysteriously humble, without identity, but personal, and timeless—also leans on the same kind of identification with an archetypal poet for its authority. Though he visited Ezra Pound at St. Elizabeth's and apprenticed himself before the modernists, and though he held the midcentury confessional poets (especially Robert Lowell and John Berryman) in the highest esteem, Merwin's real influences are much older: Homer, the troubadours, ancient Chinese and Japanese poets, the many voices of the Bible, the authors of anonymous religious and spiritual texts dug out of the earth. These are the kinds of sources Merwin wants us to align with his voice.

While other contemporaries—John Ashbery, Sylvia Plath, and Adrienne Rich among them—were relentlessly making it new, Merwin has been making it old for decades. Merwin feels blessedly out of time in our era. Despite many imitators, no one else has quite succeeded in writing like he does.

2.

Merwin has sought places out of time since his first books. But, back then, it took him a while to write his way toward the solemn authority he was after. "Tower," the first poem in *The Dancing Bears*, is nineteen quatrains long, taking most of that length to shed some of its heavy, Pre-Raphaelite ornamentation to arrive at the kind of Zen simplicity Merwin can now achieve in three lines. Near the end are these beautiful, if too-decorated, stanzas:

And my head, drifting
Bereft of body, gave me
Again from every stone
My astonishment.

A pebble might have rung
A crash of seven years' portent
On that water falling.
Or turn away the face.

But there was enough of portent
Folding that stony bobbin
If the failing light could limn
And limb such legerdemain.

And what if all motion
Were a web into that stance
And all shattering
But served that severance?

How lovely that fourth stanza above is, abstract and yet vivid, a descriptive contradiction Merwin has mastered. But did the poem really demand the head be "Bereft of body"? It's a bit much, a bit formal, a bit, well, *poetic*. Perhaps Merwin still suffers from this striving toward wisdom and profundity to this day, but he hits his mark so often (so much more often than most poets) that it's hard to fault him for aiming for it, even if his stance sometimes puts on airs.

There is, on the one hand, so much richness in this early work, a poet harvesting his fertile imagination—he seemed flooded with poetry, publishing new books every two or three years. But, so much of the early work is needlessly convoluted, backward, overdone:

The bear had gone. She touched a silver bell.
She stood straightway in a white chamber
By a bed of lapis lazuli. Red agate
And yellow chrysolite the floors. A white
Carnelian window gave upon cut hills
Of amethyst and yellow serpentine
Pretending summer; when she stood naked there
Her nakedness from the lighted stones
Sprang a thousand times as a girl or woman,
Child or staring hag. The lamps went black;

When she lay down to sleep, a young man came
Who stayed all night in the dark beside her
But was gone before dawn came to that country.

This is a typical stanza from "East of the Sun and West of the Moon," a long poem from Merwin's second collection that seems to have stolen many moves from Dante Gabriel Rossetti's playbook. Really? The window "gave upon" the hills? And the hills were "pretending summer"? It just seems needlessly out of step. Yet, of course, there is something Merwin's after that he catches with these effects. It's the same timeless power as his Pre-Raphaelite forebears found in their willfully hyperrealistic canvases and poems about myths and fantasies, but the problem is they got there first, more than half a century before. Of course, Merwin's lines about how "her nakedness . . . / Sprang a thousand times" from "lighted stones" are absolutely extraordinary, and there are many more like them to make the poem well worth reading. It indicates the extreme effort Merwin was undertaking to grow as an artist, to extend the range of his voice.

How did he journey from these odd artifacts to the seemingly artless style of the recent books? In *The Moving Target*, Merwin's mature style fitfully takes shape, wrestling with his older manner for control:

No need to break the mirror.
Here is the face shattered,
Good for seven years of sorrow.

This three-line poem, called "Economy," is an early example of gesturing toward the Asian poetry that Merwin read and loved early on and has translated throughout his career. Already evident is the stripped-down simplicity that has come to define Merwin's late style, and the sudden, soft-landing leap that is Merwin's version of epiphany.

Later in the same collection, in "To Where We Are," Merwin has already dropped most of his punctuation, using only end stops and line breaks to cork his thoughts:

With open arms the water runs in to the wheel.

I come back to where I have never been.
You arrive to join me.
We have the date in our hands.

We come on to where we are, laughing to think
Of the Simplicities in their shapeless hats
With a door so they can sit outside it

I hope I may say
Our neighbors
Natives of now, creatures of
One song,
Their first, their last,

Listen.

That "date in our hands" is much bigger than a handful. It's the kind of symbol Merwin likes: open, poignant, reaching back to an unrecorded time. He is also developing his signature line, an organic expression of a thought, variable in length, using breath as a measure and the eye for emphasis.

But, it is in 1967's *The Lice* that Merwin finds his true and lasting voice, the one he is still mining. "The Last One" is one of my favorite poems of all time, and I'd say one of the finest poems written in the 1960s. It encompasses a huge, grim, expanding space, channeling Merwin's increasingly articulate rage at the immoral-ity of war and humanity's selfish destruction of nature. But it's not merely a poem with an agenda, a poem with—God forbid!—a message. It is a space in which history, current events, and emotion swirl into myth:

> Well they'd made up their minds to be everywhere because why not.
> Everywhere was theirs because they thought so.
> They with two leaves they whom the birds despise.
> In the middle of stones they made up their minds.
> They started to cut.
>
> Well they cut everything because why not.
> Everything was theirs because they thought so.
> It fell into its shadows and they took both away.
> Some to have some for burning.
>
> Well cutting everything they came to the water.
> They came to the end of the day there was one left standing.
> They would cut it tomorrow they went away.
> The night gathered in the last branches.
> The shadow of the night gathered in the shadow on the water.
> The night and the shadow put on the same head.
> And it said Now.

I love the dark swagger of "well" and "because why not." In this poem and the others in *The Lice*, Merwin has stepped wholly out of the Victorian era, and, in the spirit of his masters William Carlos Williams and Pound, found a permanent expression of the language of his time. In the culture of the 1960s, a wish for a less mediated relationship with the earth and other people collided with unavoidable dismay at the politics and vagaries of that decade. Merwin stood up to become one of that era's principal bards, and he kept it up into the early '70s through his Pulitzer-winning *The Carrier of Ladders*. These four books, collected in *The Second Four Books of Poems* and representing his early middle period, are his most important and enduring.

3.

Merwin sustained his power through his many books published between the 1970s and '90s—*The Vixen* is one extraordinary example. His fables, published in two separate books in the '70s and now republished as *The Book of Fables*, are among the finest examples of the form since Grimm. But, in this mature work, Merwin also begins to show a vanity, perhaps a natural result of the authority he cultivated, that undermines his wisdom. The flaw in Merwin's poetry is a kind of self-importance that grows tiring, a too-obvious pleasure the poems seem to take in the sound of their own voice, the vanity of the wise. This is the risk in writing what one might call "wisdom poetry": the poet's belief that whatever he utters is worth hearing. There is an overabundance of this quality in Merwin's 1999 collection *The River Sound*. The shockingly long-winded opening poem mourns the end of Merwin's index finger, lost in an accident:

> let us be at peace with each other let peace be what is between us
>   and you now single vanished part of my left hand bit of bone
>   finger-end index
>   who began with me in the dark that was already my mother
>   you who touched whatever I could touch of the beginning
>   and were how I touched and who remembered the sense of it
>   when I thought I had forgotten it you in whom it waited
>   under your only map of one untrodden mountain
>   you who did as well as we could through all the hours at the piano
>   and who helped undo the bras and found our way to the treasure

I don't share the poem's grief over the lost digit "who helped undo the bras." Calling what's beneath them "the treasure" is simply bad, even disrespectful, writing. Merwin gets lost in the myth he makes of himself and, elsewhere in this book, of his friends in his poetic generation.

"Lament for the Makers" pays tribute to those friends and mentors in awkward rhyming quatrains, a form borrowed from William Dunbar's famous poem of the same title:

> Sylvia Plath then took her own
> direction into the unknown
>   from her last stars and poetry
>   in the house a few blocks from me
>
> Williams a little afterwards
> was carried off by the black rapids
>   that flowed through Paterson as he
>   said and their rushing sound is in me

It's a bad sign, a symptom of solipsism, when a poem ostensibly about other people ends each stanza with the word "me." Merwin seems not to realize that his friends and mentors are straw men and women holding up mirrors.

Merwin is most at home in his own free forms. When he tries something rhymey and rigid like this it feels awkward, as if he's doing a bad impression of another poet. The long poem "Testimony," which is the centerpiece of this book and name-checks every poetic peer Merwin can think of, is windy, utterly self-indulgent, and frankly terrible. This is the worst of Merwin, a kind of backsliding or straining for authority and importance, a confusion of poetic subjects— the great dead, one's great friends—for poetry. Merwin's effortless lucidity seems to have failed him for a while.

4.

Present Company, a transitional book to get between the par-for-the-course work of *The Pupil* (which, in retrospect, looks to have been Merwin's way of taking in the bagginess of *The River Sound*) and the masterful late poems of *The Shadow of Sirius*, provides ample evidence that, even going through his motions, Merwin can make good poetry out of very little. He hardly needs a subject, unlike Plath, whose breakthrough arrived when she found subjects to match her technique. In these poems, he merely needs an addressee—all the poems of *Present Company* are addressed to abstractions or at least to things that don't talk back, for example, "To Age," "To the Dust of the Road," and "To Waiting":

> You spend so much of your time
> expecting to become
> someone else
> always someone
> who will be different
> someone to whom a moment
> whatever moment it may be
> at last has come
> and who has been
> met and transformed
> into no longer being you
> and so has forgotten you

There's that slow, surprising unfolding of thought across the lines, such that the eye splashes into little epiphanies upon landing on a new line, as happens between "whatever moment it may be" and "at last has come." This is an everyday poem, not the kind of extraordinary or transcendent work Merwin is capable of at his best, but better by far than the average poem you'll meet on the street.

The late poems of *The Shadow of Sirius* are among Merwin's best. They feel effortless, like late Stevens. Merwin has synthesized his various strains, learning most deeply from the controlled storms of *The Lice*, and moved on from the backsliding of *The River Sound*, and relaxed into his late style. Almost all of the time in this book (though not in all of his late books), Merwin can step out of his own way and let the poem come through unobstructed, but with bits of his knowledge and experience clinging like soil to roots. Merwin casts his eye across time, seemingly able to remember what he himself never experienced. It's the kind of dark thrill one can only have in a poem:

> So this is the way the night tastes
> one at a time
> not early or late
>
> my mother told me
> that I was not afraid of the dark
> and when I looked it was true
> how did she know
> so long ago
>
> with her father dead
> almost before she could remember
> and her mother following him
> not long after
> and then her grandmother
> who had brought her up
> and a little later
> her only brother
> and then her firstborn
> gone as soon

as he was born
she knew

If, in his early experiments in the 1960s, punctuation seemed to be missing from the poems, now it feels as if it could never have been there, was never necessary. The stops and starts are somehow contained within the lines, if not the words themselves. Merwin locates himself in an ongoing stream of losses; the poem takes a wide view of time, the kind of wide view one would need a lifetime to take. Merwin's oracular, timeless tone has finally found its place in time. As a young man, he wrote poems wearing an old man's mask. As an old man, he's grown into that mask, such that one can no longer detect where it is fastened.

There are marvelous figures for death in these poems: "when the pictures set sail from the walls / with their lights out / unmooring without hesitation or stars / they carry no questions." He is also able to write about poetry, which figures a longing for what words refer to: "today nothing is missing / except the word for it / the morning is too / beautiful to be anything else." As he writes in a minor but telling poem, "it is the late poems / that are made of words / that have come the whole way / they have been there."

5.

In *The Moon Before Sunrise*, words seem to just come at Merwin's beckoning. The themes are the same as those in *The Shadow of Sirius*—memory, the passage of time, old age, mortality, and a sense of empathy with natural processes—but here, the work feels more solipsistic, the voice blocked by its own shadow. Merwin's work is subject to an aperture that opens and closes, letting in more and less of the world, confining him to his own vision, or transcending it.

In the past two decades, Merwin has alternated between these two states. *The Vixen* was an open book; *The River Sound* was closed; *The Pupil* was closed; *Present Company* served to help Merwin open back up again; and *The Shadow of Sirius* found him fully open and receptive. *The Moon Before Sunrise* finds him closing again, even though the subjects seem as expansive as ever. Nature in this book is nature through the scrim of Merwin, nature with Merwin blocking some of the view. The best poems here take as their subjects that specific occlusion, where what're mourned are the parts of the past that the self prevents itself from seeing:

> Youth is gone from the place where I was young
> even the language that I heard here once
> its cadences that went on echoing
> a youth forgotten and the great singing
> of the beginning have fallen silent
> with the voices that were the spirit of them
> and their absences were no more noticed
> than were those of the unreturning birds
> each spring until there were no words at all
> for what was gone but it was always so
> I have no way of telling what I miss
> I am the only one who misses it

So why does this happen? How does a poet as powerful and capacious as Merwin come to imitate himself? By now, Merwin has attained something like what Stevens had by the end, as in "The River of Rivers in Connecticut":

> It is the third commonness with light and air,
> A curriculum, a vigor, a local abstraction . . .
> Call it, once more, a river, an unnamed flowing,

Space-filled, reflecting the seasons, the folk-lore
Of each of the senses; call it, again and again,
The river that flows nowhere, like a sea.

This is not a description of a river, but an imaginary place with a
real river in it, one that has flowed through Stevens and comes out
in the poem. Stevens has taken his Connecticut landscape into
himself and filled his words with it, changing Connecticut a tiny
bit in the process. By the time he wrote this, Stevens was an absolute virtuoso of Stevens's style, such that he could play his own
instrument as well as could be imagined, but also such that he
couldn't help but imitate himself. Something similar has happened
to Merwin. His body of work is unusual in that he had a long and
fruitful middle period, a series of books in the 1960s and '70s that,
finally, represent his most lasting and important work.

In many ways, Merwin has struggled to overcome or proceed
onward from the greatness of his middle period. It's hard not to
see many of the poems in the '80s, '90s, and 2000s as echoes
of poems from *The Lice* and *The Carrier of Ladders*—or echoes
of those *kinds* of poems. Much of the later work stands in the
shadow of the middle poems. Merwin, like William Wordsworth,
has had a long career that includes many kinds of development:
surges, plateaus, and even regressions. But few poets get this good
at writing like themselves, and there are many poems—especially
in *Present Company* and *The Shadow of Sirius*—that are incredible
examples of poetry written with the kind of calm wisdom and authority that only a poet like late Stevens and Merwin, who are
perfectly at home in their own voices, could have written. Few
poets get to write so deeply through a whole life, a whole era, as
Merwin has.

3. ENDING
and
ENDURING

Rehearsals and Rehashings

1.

Many—perhaps most—poets only struggle with one or two principal themes or questions or concerns throughout their writing lives, altering their approach, perhaps coming closer, seeing more clearly, in successive poems. A very few great poets have wider purviews. Still, sometimes early poems come to seem like drafts of, or rehearsals for, later ones, though this implies that the later poems are "better," which is not necessarily the case; in many instances, they are wiser, or perhaps sobered, disheartened, by a lifetime's experiences. Sometimes the late poems attempt answers to the earlier poems' questions; other times, they admit defeat and finally abandon the pursuit of an answer, or of answers in general. But these poems that are versions of one another are remarkable glimpses into how their authors grew, showing where the rhetorical journey begins and where it leads, if not where it ends.

The classic example of poetic recapitulation may be in W. B. Yeats. As one of the truly major poets of the English language, his interests, obsessions, and capacities are far too varied and wide-ranging to have been stated and revisited in any single pair of poems. But, he began in the late nineteenth century with the intention to create a revitalized mythology for the Irish culture, and that remained one of his aims to the end. One of his very late poems, the extraordinary "The Circus Animals' Desertion," published in 1939, is one of the most powerful examples of a revisitation and extension, even closure, of a life's work in poetry. In it, he bids farewell to, and mourns the loss of, many of his creations and metaphors, resigning himself to what he discovers is the dark final resting place of all imaginative life: "The foul rag and bone shop of the heart," yet another of his enduring figures.

The roots of that poem extend everywhere throughout Yeats's body of work, and we can certainly dig them up in the first poem of his first book, "The Song of the Happy Shepherd." Yeats was among the last Romantics and the first Moderns, passing through the advent of modernism, modernizing to an extent, but never giving up the older world of poetry in which he began. So the poet has "ruth" and "sooth," though these old-fashioned words really recall a much older tradition that the modernizing Yeats wishes to evoke for the poem's purposes. But, Yeats begins and ends his career with poems of mourning for lost realms of imagination: the first one begins lamenting how "The woods of Arcady are dead, / And over is their antique joy; / Of old the world on dreaming fed; / Grey Truth is now her painted toy." The same lament is recapitulated in "The Circus Animals' Desertion," in which Yeats asks, "What can I but enumerate old themes"?

He goes on to list a bunch of them, his "circus animals," and then to grieve how little his work ultimately comes to. There's "that sea-rider Oisin led by the nose / Through three enchanted islands, allegorical dreams"; and *The Countess Cathleen,*" "pity-crazed, had given her soul away / But masterful Heaven had intervened to save it"; and "Cuchulain [who] fought the ungovernable sea." Finally, though, despite the enduring dramas he created in poetry, plays, and prose, "masterful images," he proudly calls them, he feels consigned to admit that art does not change the world, because,

> . . . when all is said
> It was the dream itself enchanted me:
> Character isolated by a deed
> To engross the present and dominate memory.
> Players and painted stage took all my love
> And not those things that they were emblems of.

Is there a more beautiful passage about the promise and uselessness of poetry? It's particularly poignant coming from a poet who wrote some of the finest political poems in the language. Here, Yeats admits, past tense, that he was more obsessed with "the dream itself"— the fantasies, metaphors, images, emblems, and words, the poet's tools—"And not those things that they were emblems of," not the world, the people, their violence, love, and hoped-for peace. Finally, he must retreat to poetry: "I must be satisfied with my heart."

Except that he's hardly making a new retreat after a lifetime's battle. The campaign began with Yeats's early admission that, as Auden would famously say in his elegy for Yeats, "poetry makes nothing happen." Way back in 1889, in "The Song of the Happy Shepherd," Yeats writes,

> Of all the many changing things
> In dreary dancing past us whirled,
> To the cracked tune that Chronos sings,
> Words alone are certain good.

Words didn't save the ancient heroes of long-ago epics: "Where are now the warring kings?" Yeats asks. "An idle word is now their glory," he answers. In fact, he goes further, warning against the futility, at least in terms of changing politics or cheating death, of the poetic career he is beginning, wary of searching "fiercely after truth, / Lest all thy toiling only breeds / New dreams, new dreams;

there is no truth / Saving in thine own heart." Decades later, stuck with his old list of "New dreams, new dreams," his "circus animals," he even uses that same word—"heart"—to name the secret place where poetry begins and ends.

Yeats's grand conclusion is not that poetry is a waste of time. Tired and daunted by old age and oncoming death, Yeats certainly inflects his late poem with sad resignation, but it's a celebration, too, albeit a dark one. Yeats names the dark glory of his poet's vocation: it is beauty, finally, that the poet pursues, whatever his subjects might have been: the dancing, descending rhythm of the poem's last two lines is Yeats at his most gorgeous—"I must lie down where all the ladders start / In the foul rag and bone shop of the heart." There's nothing foul about that music—when the final rhyme rings, though it marks the poem's resigned conclusion, this "heart" does indeed feel like a "start," a taking-off point, like the command toward the end of "The Song of the Happy Shepherd": "dream thou!"

2.

Sylvia Plath wrote poems about what she called in her journals "the old father-worship subject" at least three times, rehearsing for her late masterpiece, "Daddy." Like the statue of "The Colossus," the image of her father, who died when she was a child, loomed over her art as much as it seems to have loomed over her actual psyche. In fact, "The Colossus," Plath's first masterpiece, is a rewrite of an even earlier poem, "Full Fathom Five," in which she treats her father-muse with far less vitality and invention, a Poseidon-like figure with "white hair, white beard, far-flung, / A dragnet, rising, falling, as waves / crest and trough." She ends this poem longing to join her father-god in the depths: "Father, this thick air is murderous. / I would breathe water."

By the time "The Colossus" comes to her in 1958, the father is still god-size, and ancient, but here he is somewhat more alive. Plath has had a profound change of mind about the father's posthumous role in her life: not only is she no longer waiting for her rescue ship's "scrape of a keel / On the blank stones of the landing," but she also no longer wishes to join a living, breathing father. By the time of "The Colossus," the father is not alive: he's a statue, a symbol, a work of art, and Plath is resigned, comforted, and a bit excited, to remain in his unreconcilable presence, huddled in his ear.

But the key change that enables her to write "Daddy" has already taken place. She's decided to allow the father to exist purely in the realm of imagination, untethered to any biographical person. In fact, she only knew her father in her childhood—he died when she was eight. In her poems, she had been edging toward an increasingly imaginary version of him. This decision is what allows her to finally conscript whatever imagery she likes—even including images, vocabulary, and characters from the Holocaust—to create the father-monster that makes "Daddy" so unforgettable, so powerful, so problematic.

Many find Plath's use of Holocaust imagery unconscionable, even though it's by that very means—taking metaphor far too far—that Plath empowers this wildly over-the-top poem. Of course, she wanted to offend her readers, to make them take notice: slumbering in her father's ear, spending eternity obsessing over him, hadn't done the trick, hadn't quite expressed how big, how self-defining this metaphor-man really was. So, she had to make him into a creature no one could stand, a "Panzer-man, panzer-man, O You."

And she had to erase the older image, too, saying "I have always been scared of *you*, / With your Luftwaffe, your gobbledygoo. / And your neat mustache / And your Aryan eye, bright blue," as though he had always been Hitler, had always been waiting to destroy her, as though it's not all of a sudden that she realizes, "I think I may well be a Jew."

As a Jew whose grandparents came to America fleeing Hitler's takeover of Austria, I have a hard time not taking this personally, but that's precisely what's always drawn me to it: Plath taught herself to find the metaphor that makes this personal. She's gone too far, but I can't help but admire the success of her communication: she's leapt out of her head, crossed time, cheated death, and pissed me off more than fifty years later. It's what all poets dream of—sticking around, preserved in the poetry—though few poets would—perhaps none should—go to these lengths to achieve it.

3.

Robert Hayden offers a particularly poignant example of a rehearsal or rehashing, of an early poem answered and completed by a late one. Hayden's fundamental subject is alienation. His poems almost always narrate experiences of not belonging; his speakers look around and recognize that they are different from those they see, that they are misunderstood by others whom they themselves also misunderstand. Of course, this is a metaphor for the condition of being black in America, for the legacy of slavery. But, more broadly, Hayden's alienated poetry describes the overall strangeness and isolation of being human, of feeling at equal removes from one's inner and outer experiences, equally cut off from the self and the world, because both finally elude the grasp of words and hands. Hayden is, in part, a Romantic poet of aloneness.

While Hayden wrote many poems—such as "Runagate Runagate" and "Middle Passage"—that movingly inhabit historical characters and moments in an effort to make the horrors of slavery press upon the present, the general theme of alienation is woven throughout his poems, no matter the outward subject. Plagued by poor vision, Hayden wore thick, thick glasses, and his poems are always conscious of a heavy pane—like a diving helmet or a space mask separating the self and the world.

Hayden opens his *Collected Poems*—which is actually his own selection of what he wished to preserve, omitting early books and many scattered poems—with a taut poem called "The Diver," in which a swimmer "Swiftly descended / into canyon of cold / night-green emptiness" toward "the dead ship," a wreck filled with "the ectoplasmic / swirl of garments, / drowned instruments / of buoyancy, / drunken shoes." This diver's view narrows, burrows, specifies, admitting only what is nearby, occluded by the "fogs of water."

"The Diver" actually begins by grammatically disorienting the reader:

> Sank through easeful
> azure. Flower
> creatures flashed and
> shimmered there—
> lost images
> fadingly remembered.

One could read this opening as a continuation of a sentence started in the title—"The Diver / Sank . . ."—but I prefer not to: Hayden is careful with his pronouns in this poem, using them sparingly. The word "I" is used only three times, though it is a first-person narrative. I like to think Hayden is strategically withholding the subject of the first sentence (and of those that follow) in order to place readers at the center of the poem's descent: without an "I" to start the sentence, readers, looking outward, become the poem's speaker, seeing everything but themselves, barred from self-description, from the inner vision enabled by an "I," permitted only to see what's ahead.

Hayden's *Collected Poems* ends with a long, late masterpiece, "[American Journal]," which comprises the imaginary notes taken by an extraterrestrial sent to Earth to observe and report back to its superiors, "The Counselors." Hayden's alien is equally awestruck and dismayed by the subject, the people of America; like the diver's blindered, zoomed-in undersea vision, the alien's satellite view prevents it from really being able to see or comprehend what's before its eyes, though it does try to get close, gathering heaps of detail, such as "parades fireworks displays video spectacles / much grandiloquence much buying and selling." These kinds of observations don't finally add up to a whole the alien can relate to. It finds itself confronted with "an organism that changes even as i / examine it   fact and fantasy never twice the / same   so many variables."

Hayden's alien wonders about "the americans   this baffling / multi people," not knowing "how / describe them"; the alien finds the subject beyond the grasp of language. So too does the diver, who attempts but does not succeed at describing "livid gesturings, / eldritch hide and / . . . laughing / faces."

Imagine these two poems as the beginning and end of a journey. It's as if, in the years between the diver's hazy exploration and the alien's admission of the indescribability of "the americans," life experience not only confirmed Hayden's feeling of distance between the self and the world but also led him to perceive, at least in his poems, that the distance had increased. It's as though the better he knew himself, the more he felt he didn't, couldn't, belong.

These two poems represent the development of how a poet treats his subject matter as well as how, formally, he renders it: "The Diver," with its three- and four-word lines, its bare, suggestive descriptions, its hidden pronouns, is the work of a poet for whom too much language risks obscuring what the words refer to. The long, verbose, speechy lines of "[American Journal]" indicate a poet now anxious that his words are not enough to describe anything adequately. But

a sad sort of wisdom has been gained: in fact, words are not suffi-
cient to bridge inner and outer lives; the promise of the dive is ultimately thwarted.

"The Diver" asks a question—why he ultimately "strove against
the / canceling arms that / suddenly surrounded / me." Why, when
he at last reaches his goal, the ship, the ostensible truth of his journey, does he feel he has to flee? The reason is not simply the diver's
"Reflex of life-wish." "[American Journal]" reaches a darker, more
final conclusion—its speaker is faced with "some thing   essence /
quiddity   i cannot penetrate or name." He is simply too far out
of his element (and, more tragically, that appropriate "element" is
also unknown, unreachable), neither of the water nor of the earth,
too alien to understand. Hayden's whole body of work can be read
as the journey toward a more precise understanding of what—and
why—he cannot understand. It represents a profound account of
a black man looking in on a society—and an art form—that will
not grant him his due authority for no other reason than his race.

4.

Elizabeth Bishop's career is bookended by a pair of poems about
surfaces that depict or reflect life. "The Map," the first poem in
North & South, Bishop's debut, is an unusual fantasy that un-
folds on a world map. "Sonnet," the last poem included in the
uncollected works in Bishop's *Complete Poems, 1927–1979*, and
published in the *New Yorker* in 1979 shortly after she died, is about
a series of objects, the last of which is a mirror, though there are
no people standing before it; its culminating action, such as there
is, proceeds from close-up observation of the kind of trick of light
that all of us see, but few of us bother to notice—a realm that is
Bishop's particular province. In fact, there are no people in either
of these poems, perhaps a state that Bishop found comforting: left

alone with the precision of her thinking, the exquisite estrangement of her vision.

Bishop, a lifelong traveler, and a kind of perpetual orphan, was always seeking other places, elsewheres, escapes. Her work attests to the feeling of never being at home anywhere; like Hayden, Bishop was a poet whose essential notion of the human experience was one of distance—from the self, from others. For Bishop, language tries and largely fails to collapse the distance between words and their referents.

"The Map" shares a strategy with "The Diver": both poems play tricks with pronouns, disorient the reader, make subjects of what in other cases would be objects. The wanderlust in Bishop's eyes brings the map to life, gives it agency of its own. Though the specter of the "map-makers" looms in the background, Bishop's map seems to make its own decisions, has its own needs and motivations: "does the land lean down to lift the sea from under, / drawing it unperturbed around itself?" It quickly becomes hard to tell whether she is more interested in these places as they exist off the map, or simply in the places drawn on the map itself, an imaginary playground. "Are they assigned, or can the countries pick their colors?" she wonders. She bestows the same kind of playful sentience on the inanimate objects that populate "Sonnet," such as "the compass needle / wobbling and wavering, / undecided." Indecision, an uncertainty about what to do next, or the wish to remain between decisions, always characterizes her poems.

In one of my favorite moments in twentieth-century poetry, Bishop conflates depiction, description, and location, making a drawing and the text upon it seem capable of editing the actual world:

The names of seashore towns run out to sea,
the names of cities cross the neighboring mountains

—the printer here experiencing the same excitement
as when emotion too far exceeds its cause.

One imagines the names of those seaside towns getting a bit wet at
the ends, or perhaps hovering above the sea like clouds gathering
moisture before a storm. And perhaps the tallest mountain peaks
scrape against the letters in the names of the nearby cities. Bishop
built an aesthetic around the idea that emotion almost always "too
far exceeds its cause": most of her poems transpire in an emotionally flat world, where people, when they speak for themselves, make
mountains out of molehills, say more than others need to know.

She found her power in holding back, in not saying, emphasiz-
ing what couldn't or shouldn't be said. The map holds ambition in
reserve, keeps people where they belong, where they're stuck, while
letting them imagine they might leave. This is what happens at the
end of "Sonnet" too: the "rainbow-bird" is really nothing, the reflected light from the mirror bevel dancing around the room. It
does what people can't, or don't, or won't, "flying wherever / it feels
like, gay!"

What is more real here, the map or the world it depicts? The
"empty mirror" and the room it's in, or the bird of light that escapes the earthbound world and its rules? Bishop's poems always
wish that the answer would be the latter, and acknowledge that it
is the former. It's why she lets the fish go at the end of that famous
poem, why her greatest losses must be contained in strict musical
repetition in "One Art." She felt deeply that poetry was the way
beyond the limits of life, not to immortality, as some other poets
thought, but to experience. Poetry, with its map that makes the
names of cities into actual landmarks, with flecks of light that can
fill the human wish for freedom, is her best answer. It may be the
only place where what we can have and what we want can calmly
coexist. Why else would we read it, or "*Write* it"?

5.

What accounts for poetic development within a poet's career is really the refinement of style—honing and mastering the verbal tools required to express a poet's few subjects—and an increasing precision about what, in fact, the subjects are. This is in the best cases, for many poets find a subject and a style early and continue to write for decades without developing either. But poetry, at its best, is a means of knowledge, a way of understanding the self and how the self sees the world beyond it. I say a "means" of knowledge because poetic knowledge isn't attained, it's only pointed toward, hopefully more and more precisely. Poetry is the medium for knowledge that cannot be attained, for what is just out of reach, the just-unsayable, unthinkable, unfeelable, which "resist the imagination almost successfully," to adapt an idea from Wallace Stevens.

And so most poets rehearse and rehash their few themes many times over the course of a writing life. Style changes to reflect growing precision about subject matter, which changes, becomes, at some level, more accurate, more true, as refined style enables the poet to express it, to know it, better.

Yeats—who *was* one of those rare, capacious poets whose subjects and modes were many—began in poetry moved by the tragic awareness that language is the only means we have of crossing the divide between inner and outer worlds, between history and the present, between "reality" and "justice," the two poles he names in *A Vision*, all of which language ultimately fails to do. What his lifelong practice of writing showed him was the extent to which—though poetry could never actually bring inner and outer together—the attempts, the characters, the words, the products of his imagination, could take on real and meaningful life of their own. The poetry itself is what he would miss, what he was already grieving as he wrote his late poems. His style developed—from oracular mythmaking in the early poems to authoritative, worldly, tragic self-expression in the later ones—as the irreconcilability of reality and justice more clearly became his subject, even as that subject continually beckoned his style toward greater precision.

Plath's deepening portrayal of the father-god that haunted her imagination was a pursuit of an unfettered expression of associations, the freedom to co-opt metaphor and imagery from wherever she needed it to render emotion concretely. She came from the repressed world of 1950s New England and she sought ways to counter it, to find verbal wildness to match the interior wildness of her imagination. As she broke out of her orderly stanzas and shapely sentences, she found her unchained middle and late poems. In the process, she came to know her father as a creature of imagination, not biography, a symbol of the unknowable—and the horrific—endlessly beckoning her, and us.

Hayden moved toward increasingly precise expression of his sense of alienation, which is, of necessity, deeply personal—for how can anyone be truly alone in company? He also speaks for many African Americans. His diver, cut off because self-enclosed, finds a truer expression in his alien, cut off because excluded, other, outside. And so his later poems became more verbose, reaching with more words toward more of the world, though finally language— "their pass word   okay"—is more a cage, an enclosure, a diver's suit, than a line that leads to the world and others to draw them closer. Diver and alien are the same person, two failed attempts at—but successful expressions of—the same tragedy. The second confirms the first.

Bishop also sought freedom she finally could not attain. The map is bound by the words that label it, just as the self is bound by the map, by geography, by the limits of distance and time. In the end, freedom was a trick of light, an illusion, though a beautiful one. Bishop's imagination was frustrated by its own limits, which are the contours of her sensibility, the elements of vocabulary, syntax, imagery, memory, and desire that make her the poet she is, whose imagination sometimes "too far exceeds" her manners and restraint.

Poets write and rewrite their poems to describe these elements to themselves, for they are, finally, what compose a poet's world, a world lived in and through language. The initiating impulse behind all poems is, perhaps, the irresistible need to *say things right*, such that, as Frost says, "they'll be hard to get rid of." Poetry begins and ends in revision, which can be a lifelong process of replacing the less-true words with truer ones. The young poets Yeats, Plath, Hayden, and Bishop did not yet know what their older selves came to know. Young, they were more idealistic and hopeful, perhaps more restrained, certainly less sure of their powers. They were less used to the language and its effects, not yet sobered by the knowledge of what a great poem can and can't accomplish. But we're lucky, I think, when poets get to write across long lives. Reading their early and late poems between the covers of one book may be as close as we'll get to seeing promise fulfilled.

Louise Glück's Steady Growth

"Whatever the truth is, to speak it is a great adventure," concludes Louise Glück's tribute to her great teacher, "On Stanley Kunitz." Most of the essay narrates an episode in which Kunitz told her flatly that a cache of new poems about which she was anxious was, in fact, terrible. It is an episode that she remembers with gratitude, not because it gave her pleasure to write badly or suffer criticism, but because, as she writes, "I wanted approval, but more than that I wanted to be heard, which is, I think, a more convincing proof of existence." Kunitz's honest appraisal of her poems made her feel heard.

This says a great deal about why Glück has developed as she has. She wrote first in an effort to prove existence, and in her late work *Faithful and Virtuous Night*, to prove, as far as one can, what comes *after* existence. Perhaps more than any other poet writing, she can be described as a truth teller without sentimentality. Glück is anything but sentimental, though she is ferociously attached to the past, to its ruthless bearing on the present. In her world, there is no escape from the pain and trauma of childhood, of youth, and, especially, of family, that microcosm in which one's existence is forever cast into doubt, the tribunal before which one is ever submitting proofs to the contrary. And yet, Glück does not merely rehearse her traumas in art; she works to connect them—to myth, to narrative, to a hedging kind of spirituality—not so much in order to transcend them, but to make of them a voice that tells the penetrating truth of one kind of human experience in late twentieth- and early twenty-first-century America, where language, rather than religion, must serve as moral mirror.

From the beginning Glück has had a melancholy and skeptical sensibility. Her delivery is always deadpan. Her poems shun excitement but court surprise, in the form of revelation. Few Glück poems do not draw back some kind of veil and expose facts that the imprecisions of language and experience would otherwise conceal. I come away from her poems wiser, though rarely happier; confirmed in my existence, but afraid of what I now know I know.

Glück has been refining, deepening, and focusing her vision for decades. She switches lenses like an eye doctor, looking through the glasses of myth, autobiography, ventriloquy, until each has nothing more to show her. Glück's long career is a document of slow, steady poetic development. We see her book by book expanding her poetic identity, discarding what is no longer useful. Each of her first four books was more ambitious than the last, then came the controlled explosion of *Ararat*, which inaugurated Glück's use of the book-length sequence in which she still writes, a suite of related poems and speakers bound by a hazy narrative; and opened up new autobiographical territory to her poetry. *The Wild Iris* is a visionary work whose energy continues through *Meadowlands* and *Vita Nova*. *The Seven Ages* is a transitional book, perhaps Glück's least focused, but it points the way for the incredible capaciousness of *Averno*, a book every bit as visionary as *The Wild Iris*. Since then, Glück has been working in a space that mixes the invention and causality of fiction and the self-revelation of confessional writing.

In her debut, *Firstborn*, Glück had already "found her voice," which really means understanding her limitations and what she might yet make of them. A poet's medium is not her whole language—for Glück, American English—but the portion of it into which she was born: the family dialect, modified, somewhat enlarged, by media, reading, decades of conversation. A voice is this received vocabulary and these habits of phrasing tuned to the particular purposes of expressing the emotions that give rise to a particular poet's poems, what might be called her inspirations. Poetry does not express life—which is why few poets actually speak like they write, why they don't only talk about the subjects of their poems; rather it expresses a sensibility: the mixture of a poet's heart, mind, and voice. Poetry is more a corral than an open field. The early poem "Silverpoint" shows that Glück has already found her defining limitations, though she deploys them in a more allegorical mode:

> My sister, by the chiming kinks
> Of the Atlantic Ocean, takes in light.
> Beyond her, wreathed in algae, links on links
> Of breakers meet and disconnect, foam through bracelets
> Of seabirds. The wind sinks. She does not feel the change
> At once. It will take time. My sister,
> Stirring briefly to arrange
> Her towel, browns like a chicken, under fire.

From the outset, Glück is fiercely observant, cold, often cruel toward her poems' speaker—someone meant to suggest herself—and toward others. This poem is typical of Glück's method: it marks a small change, a young girl tanning, that becomes emblematic of a bigger one, the growth and perhaps diminishment of a person: the sister who "takes in light" is covetous of experience, wants to grow up, be, perhaps, beautiful, coveted. The world is disinterested in her—"Beyond her, wreathed in algae, links on links / Of breakers meet and disconnect"—and ultimately, she is cooked by it, "under fire," before the harsh gaze of the speaker. Glück's world is as unforgiving as her voice, simple, indifferent, unsparing. This unornamented voice is a metaphor for the world it describes.

Later, in *The Wild Iris* in one of several poems titled "Matins," Glück will warn against looking everywhere for meaning: "the happy heart / wanders the garden like a falling leaf, a figure for / the part, not the whole." This, I think, is one of the keys to Glück's poetic power, and an explanation of the unhappiness of most of the poems: while her voice is an expression of limitation, the poet-speaker of her writing looks toward "the whole" for meaning, sees everything as potentially metaphoric—the sun tanning her sister in "Silverpoint," a tree that she's climbed in "Matins." Her mind's eye charges anything observable with meaning, and this grates against her belief that the world is mostly meaningless, mostly uncaring, as she admits in the opening poem of *Ararat*:

> I was born to a vocation:
> to bear witness
> to the great mysteries.
> Now that I've seen both
> birth and death, I know
> to the dark nature of these
> are proofs, not
> mysteries—

Her "vocation" demands open, unbudging eyes "to bear witness." Her experience—"I've seen both / birth and death"—tells her that open eyes will see great disappointment, an awareness of what she calls "the dark nature" of the world.

She finds that "dark nature" in the midst of life, too, not just at its beginning and end. This is not to say Glück is merely a depressing poet, but that her worldview is consistent in the poems; the darkness is what she comes to poetry to express—Glück's actual personal life is not our, or the poems', business. But, in the poems, life's pleasure often conceals its pain, as in the shocking opening of her famous "Mock Orange":

It is not the moon, I tell you.
It is these flowers
lighting the yard.

I hate them.
I hate them as I hate sex,
the man's mouth
sealing my mouth, the man's
paralyzing body—

and the cry that always escapes,
the low, humiliating
premise of union—

There is in an echo of Sylvia Plath's "Tulips" here, the flower as intruder, and her desire to escape the "little smiling hooks" of her family, but Glück is not after numbness and escape. She doesn't ask the words to bring her relief and consolation; she simply wants the facts heard: people think sex is fun; it is not, it is violent, embarrassing, subjugating, or it can be. She closes the poem with two questions no one can answer: "How can I rest? / How can I be content / when there is still / that odor in the world?" It is precisely accurate to admit that there is no putting to rest our deepest, most disturbing questions. Glück is nothing if not accurate.

The breakthrough in *Ararat* is one of subject matter and form, the discovery of greater access to autobiography and the book-length sequence. In the poem "A Novel," Glück merges fiction and fact, makes them inextricable, because it is through the imagination that she can see accurately the emotions and drama of a life, which, in itself, is without a drama: "No one could write a novel about this family: / too many similar characters. Besides, they're all women; / there was only one hero." This hero was the father, now dead, leaving behind a mother and two sisters. In Glück's real life, she notes, "there's no plot without a hero." As an artist, Glück is interested in imbuing experience with plot, the drama, without which there is no truth. The plot overarching her body of work is the quest to disprove the existence of the plot in experience. So, in this book, she begins to make life into a fiction, one that seems to hug her biography tightly, but departs from it in notable ways, into the territory of ancient Greek and Roman myth, for instance. She expands this technique throughout her career.

Her next book, a masterpiece, is *The Wild Iris*, in which she speaks through plants and flowers, alternating these voices, which are souls returned from the beyond, angels of a sort, who deliver messages, with a divine speaker, a cold god. These visitations are interspersed with day-to-day reportage from her life, and prayers.

The flowers embody human qualities, or, in acting flowerlike, they offer alternate ways of seeing human experience, their own kinds of solutions to human problems:

> I did not expect to survive,
> earth suppressing me. I didn't expect
> to waken again, to feel
> in damp earth my body
> able to respond again, remembering
> after so long how to open again
> in the cold light
> of earliest spring—

afraid, yes, but among you again
crying yes risk joy

in the raw wind of the new world.

The flower pushing up through the earth in a new spring is an obvious figure for a person surviving and reconstituting after a tragedy. The flowers offer generous answers to the beseeching voice of the prayer poems—all titled "Matins" or "Vespers"—which argue with God: "You must see / it is useless to us, this silence that promotes belief / you must be all things, the foxglove and the hawthorn tree, the vulnerable rose and tough daisy—we are left to think / you couldn't possibly exist." When God does answer— "After all things occurred to me, / the void occurred to me"— the voice is almost toneless. One can read *The Wild Iris* as a single poem in parts, the triangulation of these three kinds of voices, whose statements, questions, and answers mostly miss each other, or at least never connect directly. It is in this vortex of voices that Glück gets as close as she can to clarity and consolation.

Also notable about *The Wild Iris* is the allowance of more breath in the poems, more words, because Glück is willing now to speak through other voices. These characters, for that is what they are, are more forgiving, sometimes more hopeful, than the Glück-poet-speaker of the earlier poems. Glück imagines a larger sensibility, allows the poems to begin telling other stories, answering for needs beyond those of her earlier speaker, who sought a context for the suffering of her family.

Fictional characters enlarge her access to "the great mysteries." By the time of *A Village Life*, after wearing the costumes drawn from "The Odyssey" in *Meadowlands*, and other mythic subjects in *Vita Nova*, *The Seven Ages*, and *Averno*, Glück is ready to assume the identities of purely made-up characters, the inhabitants of an archetypal village where "All the roads . . . unite at the fountain" and "In summer, couples sit at the pool's edge. / There's room at the pool for many reflections." Showing these many reflections in poems, Glück writes about the men, women, and children who live ordinary lives in her fictional village—an adolescent girl being given a lecture by her mother "about what she referred to as *pleasure*"; couples falling in love; the old lamenting their lost beauty and youth. At times she speaks from on high, a watchful deity, sad for her creations: "No one really understands / the savagery of this place," she says, "the way it kills people for no reason." Elsewhere, she inhabits her villagers' minds and voices, though really, the voice is always the same: it is Glück, whose verbal knife is sharpened by what suffering promises to give and take away.

Most often, she is interested in the flowering and waning of bodies. She shows teenagers discovering sex—"More and more that summer we understood / that something was going to happen to us / that would change us"; marriages ebbing into estrangement— "Your mother and I used to drink a glass of wine together / after dinner," a father tells his daughter; and beauty's final fading—"it is not the earth I will miss," a woman says to her body, "it is you I will miss." For the first time in her poems, Glück lets her lines—which were always clipped and breathless—go long, lets her sentences fill with air. In so doing, she proves that her unflinching intensity is like a gas expanding to fill its suddenly larger container.

In *Faithful and Virtuous Night*, Glück creates a future fiction extrapolated from her own past: a male version of the autobiographical *Ararat*'s daughter, a painter rather than a poet, an artist who can look ahead toward dying—directly *at* dying—with the same cold gaze she has trained on her own past. To see death—which is, of necessity, beyond the view of the dying—as a fact, Glück extrapolates and invents rather than records or remembers. She turns to allegory, to a self not unlike herself but specifically not herself.

This inverted mirror-self and its capacity to observe and character-ize becomes her mature expression.

This book is like a novel in its short vignettes with lines instead of paragraphs, though Glück's language is tense, careful as ever, not prose. She tries some technical tricks here, nothing revolution-ary as far as poetry goes, but new for her: multipage sequences of numbered parts with different stanza shapes; poems of many un-broken pages; prose poems and fables. She synthesizes all her earlier concerns, creates a fiction that mirrors and yet carefully contradicts her biography, and creates a searing confrontation with death. It is a kind of career masterwork, a recapitulation, almost a summary.

The poems all have a dreamlike quality, hinting at befores and afters to which we do not have access. This suggests the portrayal of memory, which is, at best, a poignant gloss of what actually happens, a summary revised in light of later events. The facts are poorly recorded, Glück asserts in the title poem, among her lon-gest ever at ten pages. Here are a couple of beautiful, scene-setting stanzas:

> The day had become unstable.
> Fissures appeared in the broad blue, or,
> more precisely, sudden black clouds
> imposed themselves on the azure background.

> Somewhere, in the far backward reaches of time,
> my mother and father
> were embarking on their last journey,
> my mother fondly kissing the new baby, my father
> throwing my brother into the air.

This vision emerges from "the far backward reaches of time," a place into which language itself reaches, drawing forth what it can. What comes up may not be what was desired, may, in fact, be nothing. The poem's "day" is destabilized by memory, by the inner life's interruption into experience—the "sudden black clouds" are projections, emblems of the speaker's parents "embarking on their last journey," adulthood, which ends in death. The baby is kissed, as if kissed good-bye; the brother is launched "into the air," separated metaphorically from the parents, who begin to recede as their children come to the fore.

In such poems, Glück has found the precise tone for someone yielding to history, who has accepted that no bright new future will be cut loose from the past. "[P]assions and sensations were . . . / set aside forever, and each night my heart / protested its future, like a small child being deprived of a favorite toy," she writes in "An Adventure." The protestation is natural: death makes no sense to the heart, whose job is to continue beating, to proceed. But the mind, the will, must counter it: "these farewells, I said, are the way of things." This is the tone of resignation, though it is not quite the tone of giving up: Glück remains interested in the phenomena of her mind's experience, no matter how disappointing. Having uttered her resignation, she proceeds bravely, with curiosity, adventure even, "a glorious knight riding into the setting sun, and my heart / . . . the steed underneath me." Death, like the rest of life's suffering and joy, is, among other things, surprising to the inner eye.

The story of *Faithful and Virtuous Night* centers on a male painter with an older brother, like and unlike Glück, a poet with a sister. The painter's parents died when he was a child—"You have no idea how shocking it is / to a small child when / something continuous stops"—and the siblings were raised by an aunt who took fastidious if slightly distant care of them in the English town where the painter lives in the collection's present after suffering some kind of breakdown. He has returned to the town to remember a long and sad life and, essentially, to await death.

Why, in order to face life's ending, does Glück wear a mask? This choice is a kind of fake-out, a misdirection, a trick played by the poet on her own mind. The mind balks at anticipating its own extinction, of course, so Glück has crafted a thin disguise to fool herself into vulnerability. It is a trick like that of *The Wild Iris*, in which Glück's god and flowers can flatly say what she herself is unable to admit. As for the mask's particulars: painting, after all, is much like poetry, as it traffics in not-quite-paraphrasable meanings, images, icons, and suggestions. And for Glück, a woman's identity pulls toward love, like the daughter searching for the father-hero in *Ararat*, or away from it, like Eurydice in *Averno*. To face death, Glück needs to escape that pull, to be alone, to become a man. Glück is recasting herself in the role of the abandoning father of *Ararat*, the "hero." Glück's male painter is the recast father now living out the daughter's part: he is abandoned rather than abandoning. It's a kind of comeuppance, a balancing of scales that can only happen in the imagination.

Nonchronological episodes from the painter's life are interspersed with short prose pieces narrating dreams, frequently involving artists in various mediums. The book as a whole operates as a fable about how artistic creation relates to lived life. Certainly, in Glück's view, art does not heal pain. It may magnify it. But more, it seems a habit native to a particular disposition, one that is unable to deny the wreckage of loss and so has developed an obsessive interest in it. Glück's truth telling has its roots in a passivity the artist must hone, the ability to observe the mind and the world working on each other, changing each other. The artist doesn't change the world; she watches it, watches her mind interpreting it. The artist's greatest sacrifice is involvement in her own life, an involvement that would prevent her from writing it or painting it.

The same sacrifice is required of the artist who wants to observe death, for which this book seeks, through its mask, an accurate figure. What does it feel like to accept death, to approach it, not without protest, but without any false hope that it might be avoided? What does dying *look* like, were one merely to look and not feel? What if, drowning, you didn't flail your limbs at all, but thought—or painted, or wrote? Glück attempted this before, in *The Wild Iris* in which she writes, in the guise of a flower, "You who do not remember / passage from the other world / I tell you I could speak again: whatever / returns from oblivion returns / to find a voice." Glück's vision of dying in "Approach of the Horizon," the climax of *Faithful and Virtuous Night*, is far more quotidian, less religious, less certain, more skeptical. It feels as accurate as possible, given that it must be imaginary; it transpires on a human scale. She has had plenty of practice by now describing what can't be seen:

> My birthday (I remember) is fast approaching.
> Perhaps the two great moments will collide
> and I will see my selves meet, coming and going—
> Of course, much of my original self
> is already dead, so a ghost would be forced
> to embrace a mutilation.
>
> The sky, alas, is still far away,
> not really visible from the bed.
> It exists now as a remote hypothesis,
> a place of freedom utterly unconstrained by reality.
> I find myself imagining the triumphs of old age,
> immaculate, visionary drawings
> made with my left hand—
> "left," also, as "remaining."

The painter has lost feeling in his right arm, his painting arm, and as it becomes impossible to create, it becomes impossible to live.

Glück imagines a kind of heaven in which life is the ideal: neither pure imagination nor pure experience, but pure. This would be heaven for someone who has stood conflicted for a lifetime at the crossroads of description and interpretation, of what happens and what it means, whose life's work has been to render, in plain, hard English, the shiftings of the inner world. "The sky, alas, is still far away," Glück writes, because death, and what might lie beyond it, is ever inaccessible to the living, is finally, imaginary. The living are offered no preview of death, and no transition to it—it comes complete, the end of, perhaps the solution to, both life and imagination.

What Glück struggles here to do is to render, vividly, what might immediately precede that change, that transfer of the self to oblivion, a place from which no poet, no matter how patient and precise, can report. No one publishes that kind of posthumous book.

Endings

And so we come to endings—late poems, last poems, lasting poems. Poets are obsessed with endings. There's nothing so powerful and moving as a great last line, which revises the entire poem that came before it, sending a bolt of lightning back up through the stanzas, zapping the reader's eyes back up to the top for another drop down the poem's bottomless pit.

Put simplistically, there are two ways to end a poem: by opening or by closing the box the poem makes, letting the poem expand after it's finished into more and more possibilities, or snapping it shut with a finality that implies that is all there is to say about that. Some late or last poems work that way too, revising or reenvisioning the entire career they cap, leaving it open to further interpretation or summarizing it and bringing the discussion to a kind of close.

Death, which is part of the cosmic stew that Emily Dickinson calls "immortality," and to which William Wordsworth implies we return after our earthly sojourn—we came here "trailing clouds of glory," he writes, and we go back to glory—has always been poets' home base, the ether or dreamscape where meaning originates and where poets hopefully live on through their poems. For poets, endings are never the end.

Three very different poets have meant a great deal to me for different reasons: Robert Lowell, Delmore Schwartz, and Lucille Clifton.

Lowell was a poet wildly entitled and enabled by authority of his old American name, cruel, famous, but the imagination with which he transformed the biographical facts of his life into poetry is a model of a supremely creative act. Schwartz undermined his own considerable genius; he remains an inspiration and a cautionary tale. Clifton was the first poet I ever saw give a reading, sometime in the mid-1990s when I was a teenager and just beginning to try to write poems. Her powerful presence is an archetype of what a poet should be.

Robert Lowell

> Those blessed structures, plot and rhyme—
> why are they no help to me now
> I want to make
> something imagined, not recalled?

Those are the first lines of Lowell's "Epilogue," the crowning poem of his final book. What a finale. How many poets are granted the wit and authority to make the final poem of their last, posthumously published book, a summary of all that has come before, pressing at the central question of their work? But that's the kind of poet Lowell was: his command was extraordinary, superhuman. It was given him to make an unparalleled autobiographical poetry, a poetry that seems to see the self, with its many flaws (not the least of which is the lashing cruelty inflicted upon his loved ones by his poetry), completely from both a bird's and a bug's eye; it's also a poetry that does not grant the self the capacity to act on its insights, to repair what it has broken. And this may be one of the sober facts of poetry, that its insights are fleeting, that it does not heal so much as envision. Poetry is not therapy: its changes happen in the language, not the writer.

In his late poems, Lowell returns, after a decade of casting and recasting countless sonnets, to a seemingly freewheeling, sloppy free verse. One feels the excitement of escaping from the stricture of the sonnet, which held him in its thrall. In "Epilogue" and other poems from Lowell's last book, the line is its own organic unit, its own meter, its own necessity in ways it could not be when he was married to the sonnet. When I feel stuck, in search of a new music for my own poems, I come back to this late Lowell and remember that poetry, with its rules and the poet's capacity to learn and then break them, has all the varied equipment one needs.

Lowell finds himself, after his long career, his sonnets, his practice, stuck in the mode of confession, really, of observation, description, and dramatization. He wants to make things up, and finds that he can't, that he doesn't know how to "make / something imagined"; he is at the mercy of the "threadbare art of my eye," too obsessed with the actual people of his life to invent anything. And that obsession got him into plenty of trouble, has left in his work, in posterity, a primer on what not to do to one's loved ones in art. His books *For Lizzie and Harriet* and *The Dolphin* describe the dissolution of Lowell's marriage to Elizabeth Hardwick, and intimately discuss their daughter; Lowell went so far as to cast Hardwick's actual letters into sonnets. Upon reading it, Lowell's friend Elizabeth Bishop wrote, horrified, "Art just isn't worth that much."

But how "threadbare" is Lowell's eye, really? And to what extent was it actually the eye that he was using to see? What Lowell did, unforgivably, was a powerful, sometimes horrendous act of imagination: he made, in his poetry, all the others he saw, into aspects of himself. No, he could not bestow "the grace of accuracy / Vermeer gave to the sun's illumination." What he did instead of describing the real world, the real sun, was to describe the self, himself, in terms of everyone he loved. That, I think, is the soul and excitement of "confessional" poetry, and why it is so misunderstood: it's projection, not reportage, a transformative, imaginative act, the recasting of the world in one's own image so that one can see oneself in it, in a mirror the size of the world, or perhaps of the poet's ego. This method, practiced well, affords accuracy, if not about the "real" outer world, then about the inner world of the poet, and the reader.

"We are poor passing facts," Lowell says, temporary, soon to be wiped from memory. But, the poem can preserve us, though at some cost. When he says we are "warned by that"—and I love that "that," a pronoun made to bear more than its share of emotional weight, an innocuous word asked here to stand in for all the temporality of human existence—the warning is not simply about how fleeting we are, but about the mortal risks of poetry. In exchange for immortality, we give up—or at least Lowell does, with his backstabbing, unforgiving sensibility—much everyday human goodness. In order to stick, poetry demands drama, something often absent in real life: things happen, they don't mean much, until we put them into a story, a completely human invention. And for Lowell, it was necessary to risk something actual—hurt to himself and others—for his poems to sing.

Narrative is the basic function of human imagination, something Lowell deeply understood. You can't show all sides of someone, the person's kindness and darkness, at one time. Lowell was always feigning ignorance of himself to create his poems. The conflict inside them is fundamentally the conflict between the observer and the storyteller, between the person who knows what happened and the one who wants to make it interesting, permanent, powerful.

That, for me, is the fundamental excitement in Lowell's poetry. To give an imagined character, an aspect of the story of oneself, "his living name," the real name, the one the real person answered to day after day, is to bravely blur a sacred line between truth and lie, action and imagination. The lie makes "what happened" stick like a choking bone in memory. The lie makes the people live forever, and isn't that what poetry is after?

I suppose one's answer to that question is also the answer to whether one can love Lowell, and forgive him. It's an unforgettable question to leave us with.

Delmore Schwartz

Preceding every poem is the same urgent need to say something and to have it acknowledged, to have some proof that what the poem says has been heard. By this measure, almost no poem succeeds: the poem offers only half of what would fulfill it; the other half resides with imaginary readers, who may never open the book, and who, if they do, will almost certainly never send acknowledgment back to the poet in ways the poet can receive. Perhaps very famous poets palpably feel the acknowledgment of their readers, but most poets rarely do, maybe only a few times in their lives. Of course, poets don't bet much on acknowledgment; what excites them is finding a precise way to say what they need, or finding out what they need in the act of saying it, and imagining the person they need to be heard by.

"The Heavy Bear Who Goes with Me," the most famous poem by Delmore Schwartz, the twentieth century's most thwarted poet, strikes me as a prime example of this principle in action. The speaker of this poem is desperate for a specific kind of feedback, a kind that the poem tries to pretend it doesn't want, but which finally it reveals its need for. Schwartz wanted, more than anything, to be famous, to be acknowledged as a genius—his letters can be excruciating, stuffed with a kind of skull-busting ambition and self-aggrandizement that renders Schwartz so big there can't possibly be room for him in the world. Finally, he sized himself out of it, dying crazed and spiteful in an obscure New York hotel, having dispatched, through his lawyer, accusatory letters to friends and others who had supported him for years.

He wanted to be big because he was direly afraid he was small, even paranoid, and perhaps his self-assessment was accurate. And in fact, in many ways, he was—unable to escape his crushing self-consciousness, his fears, his frustrations, his hopes. His poems and stories, and letters and journals testify to that in abundance. As does the wreckage of spent friendships he left behind him.

I'm indulging deeply here in the suspicious act of reading a poet's biography into his poems, because, with Schwartz, as with Lowell, the poems are enlarged by the roiling of his personality; they are justified, explained. Schwartz hoped his poems would make up for him, excuse a lifetime's bad behavior in eternity, and because he encoded that hope in the poems themselves—nowhere more than in "The Heavy Bear Who Goes with Me"—they do:

> The heavy bear who goes with me,
> A manifold honey to smear his face,
> Clumsy and lumbering here and there,
> The central ton of every place,
> The hungry beating brutish one
> In love with candy, anger, and sleep,
> Crazy factotum, dishevelling all,
> Climbs the building, kicks the football,
> Boxes his brother in the hate-ridden city.

There is a lumbering, blunt, over-the-head quality to these lines. The pieces—the words—that make up the poem are big, unsubtle, bricks rather than feathers. "The central ton of every place" can't be missed; it takes up most of wherever it is. There is wonderful, clumsy bearishness to this poem, and to many of Schwartz's—this is the poem in which he teaches himself and us how to read him: "face" rhymes obviously with "place"; the bear "climbs the building," any building, because one is as good as another for this purpose—the bear does what he shouldn't, gets in the way, doesn't control himself.

How lucky to have "a swollen shadow" to whom to outsource one's sins, not even an evil twin, but someone who looks different, who looks not like you, not even like an evil you, but like evil. What is a bear? What do we think of when we think of "bear"? Play dead if you see one. Against his fury, there is nothing anyone can do. What a perfect figure he is. Because, of course, there is also the circus bear, "A stupid clown of the spirit's motive," a monster in a skirt balancing on a ball, the anger trained out of it, forgotten, ridiculous, without even the dignity its fearsome body should command.

Schwartz embarrasses himself, "Dressed in his dress-suit, bulging his pants"—oh, how I love Schwartz's misuse of verbs, "bulging" made active, and odd and active "mouthing" suddenly a creepy descriptor. The bear "Howls in his sleep for a world of sugar," the glutton, and shows himself to be no more than "quivering meat." He is a jealous, threatening monster too, one who "Stretches to embrace the very dear / With whom I would walk without him near." Those lines capture exactly the shame and pride that are everywhere in this poem, the imprisonment and the power. Look how the rhymes shackle the bear to the girl—"dear" and "near" are almost the same word—and the man to his bear. The rhyme leaves no way out of the fact of those lines, but the cage bars ring with music.

There's dignity and indulgent beauty in the phrasing. The lines "That inescapable animal walks with me, / Has followed me since the black womb held" remind me of nothing more than the verbal lavishness of Dylan Thomas's masterpiece of dark luxury, "Lament," which begins, "When I was a windy boy and a bit / And the black spit of the chapel fold / (Sighed the old ram rod, dying of women)." Schwartz aspired to that kind of music, the reader's payoff for enduring the writer's embarrassment and shame.

So why does he drag himself through the mud this way, and why so beautifully? I taught this poem to a class of undergraduates along with the poem "Wild Geese" by Mary Oliver, a poem that was a teenage lifeline to me, though I now find it oversimplifies its central problem. It's a kind of ridiculous pairing, but my theme was self-love and self-hate. Photocopied on opposite sides of the same sheet, the two poems seem made to answer one another. Schwartz's "beating brutish one" confesses right off to "[Boxing] his brother in the hate-ridden city." Oliver answers with foregone forgiveness: "You do not have to be good." I'll wager Schwartz's is the better poem, but Oliver's sentiment is what Schwartz wants in return. Though a few of my students found Oliver's poem baiting—"Tell me about despair, yours, and I will tell you mine"—I think Oliver offers that in order to make whoever "you" are feel more normal and comfortable, feel among friends who also feel despair. Schwartz offers no such trade. He wants to tell his despair, but is not here to listen to yours. He's not here at all, and his poem understands that in a way Oliver's isn't meant to. The poem is a megaphone, not a telephone, operating in one direction only. It must accomplish what it hopes to accomplish without having to hear back from the reader.

What can a poem accomplish simply by being read, by being tolerated, even enjoyed until the end? Why do any of us confess the wrong we have done? What do we want in return? Forgiveness, of course, as I said. But what's so remarkable about Schwartz's poem is the way it gets what it needs: by reading it, enjoying it, singing and savoring its music, don't we forgive it? Aren't we implicitly admitting that this bear, this Delmore Schwartz, has his powerful charms? All we have to do is get to the bottom of the page, and Schwartz is forgiven his whole miserable life.

Lucille Clifton

I wonder if poetry readers who first encounter Lucille Clifton's extraordinary poetry now, posthumously, in the magisterial *Collected Poems* edited by Kevin Young and Michael S. Glaser, will understand the awe she inspired in the late phases of her career. She was more than a writer—she was a seer, a timeless vision of The Poet who radiated, in her presence as much as in her poems, a force that could only be called wisdom. Or so she seemed to me when I first saw her read in Katonah, New York, in 1995, and so she has always seemed since. I was fifteen, rapidly descending into the depths of my young grief over my mother's death the previous year, and desperately searching for a way forward, for a hopeful notion of the life that might await me. My eleventh-grade English teacher took my class to this reading of a poet I'd never heard of before, and it was one of those few events in my life that I can say with certainty changed me forever.

I'm sure those who knew her personally saw other, less elevated sides of her, but the poet I saw from my seat in the audience shone with grace, certainty, power, and humility all at once. And what was most remarkable to me, what changed me, was that all this energy coming from her seemed to originate in language, had its source in her words, which sounded older and more permanent than her, than any person.

Fresh from a battle with breast cancer and about to publish her collection *The Terrible Stories*, she read, among other poems, "lumpectomy eve," which speaks of

> the lonely nipple

> lost in loss and the need
> to feed that turns at last
> on itself   that will kill

> its body for its hunger's sake
> all night i hear the whispering
> the soft

> love calls you to this knife
> for love   for love

> all night it is the one breast
> comforting the other

Knowing nothing then of cancer nor of the complex and compromised hopes that can shape adulthood, and still harboring, in spite, or perhaps because of my mother's death, an overdramatic view of mortality, I nonetheless immediately recognized this poem's impossible combination of consolation and resolve. Here was a voice that could rage at and grieve and even pity the decay and betrayal of the body and the fragility of life—"the need / to feed that turns at last / on itself   that will kill // its body for its hunger's sake"—and, in the same long breath, accept the loss with generous dignity: "love calls you to this knife." I knew I needed a voice like that, one I could hear and be nurtured by, and one with which, ultimately, I could write. This was the true possibility of poetry—conflicting feelings felt together, spoken in the same sentence.

Clifton's body of work is filled, end to end, over hundreds of pages, with poems like this, from her early political pieces that claim power in poverty and marginalization in America—such as "in the inner city"—to her visionary late elegies to herself and to life: "i saw a small moon rise / from the breast of a woman / lying in a hospital hall / and I saw that the moon was me" ("dying").

This is medicine that doesn't pretend to cure, but that helps one to live nonetheless. This is literature, language transformed into the living, breathing stuff of humanity. For Clifton, each word is a talisman, a bridge to the deep history of human utterance and feeling. Her unpunctuated and uncapitalized sentences, like Merwin's, suggest the immemorial origins of language, the syllables that preceded the conventions of periods and commas, that predate the splintering of Language into languages. Clifton's poems remind me that, despite all that we don't have in common, all that separates us—age, race, gender—we are related, or should aspire to be; that's an aspiration that perhaps only poetry is capable of achieving.

"In the middle of the Eye" is the last poem in Clifton's *Collected Poems*, and it's a fitting final note for this great poet to sing:

> In the middle of the Eye,
> not knowing whether to call it
> devil or God
> I asked how to be brave
> and the thunder answered,
> "Stand. Accept." so I stood
> and I stood and withstood
> the fiery sight.

Kevin Young writes that this tiny poem "appears to be the last poem Clifton wrote," found in her daybook from February 2010, the month she died. Only a few poets give themselves such a prescient send-off or so exact a summary of the total meaning of their work. "I asked how to be brave," Clifton writes, "and the thunder answered, / 'Stand. Accept.' so I stood / and I stood and withstood / the fiery sight." Yes, she was brave enough to "Stand [and] Accept," and to articulate and transform the trials of a fully lived life. But this poem is not self-congratulatory, nor, quite, is it humble. "The fiery sight" she withstood was her own—the consequence of her lifelong choice to keep her eyes and heart open and her pen moving. This is what poets sign up for, though few uphold that contract to the end. The best of them can't ever die.

Acknowledgments

These essays, in whole or in part, appeared, in very different versions, in the following publications:

American Poetry Review, American Poets, Boston Review, Cleveland Plain Dealer, Los Angeles Review of Books, NPR, *The Paris Review Daily, Poetry, Poetry Ireland Review*, and *The Yale Review*.

I'd like to thank Jeff Shotts of Graywolf Press for summoning this book into being, and everyone else at Graywolf for their hard work and care, Steph Burt for help and an utterly inspiring example, Gabrielle Calvocoressi for encouraging me to write some of these essays, my students for inspiring so much of the thinking that went into this book, Kevin Prufer for many things, including his long-ago essay on the "genre" of first books, Mary Otto for taking me to that Lucille Clifon reading, the Catwalk Institute and Denniston Hill for time and space to write, all the poets living and dead whose work has given so much to me and to others, and, of course, Brenda for, among other things, the "birthday door" behind which I was able to finish this book.

Permissions

© Sarah Tew

Craig Morgan Teicher is the author of three collections of poems, most recently *The Trembling Answers*; and a collection of stories and fables, *Cradle Book*. He edited *Once and for All: The Best of Delmore Schwartz*. He writes about books regularly for many publications, including the *New York Times Book Review*, the *Los Angeles Times*, and NPR. He has taught at NYU, the Iowa Writers' Workshop, and Princeton University, works at *Publishers Weekly*, and lives in New Jersey with his wife and children.

The text of *We Begin in Gladness* is set in Adobe Garamond Pro. Book design by Rachel Holscher. Composition by Bookmobile Design & Digital Publisher Services, Minneapolis, Minnesota. Manufactured by Versa Press on acid-free, 30 percent postconsumer wastepaper.